From Suffering to Soaring

Richard N. Schooping

A Pebble Thrown Publishing
www.richardschooping.com

ISBN 978-0-578-00525-6

First Edition
Printed in the USA

Welcome, I am overjoyed to share my first book with you. It is my honor to humbly share my transcendent journey in, out, and beyond AIDS, or beyond what I call *AIDS Consciousness.*

I was not sure when or if this writing would ever occur as this book has been a long time coming. The storms in my life have been successive. Seems I was determined to find the jetties, and that I did. And it is not easy to write in a tempest as the pages and days fly everywhere in the storm. But In the following calm all became clear and now here are my words.

This book has been a cathartic experience in that I had started writing with the intention of creating a book a few times over the past years but each draft fizzled and faded before its completion. During other renditions as I wrote I would find that I was still emotionally and energetically connected to the past. I was not flowing, and so as I wrote I experienced the energies of my yesterdays and lost inspiration. My body would actually physically hurt or cry as I wrote. I would know and feel such a memory that for days after writing a certain chapter I was depressed, moody, or even angry. Then I would without intention stop writing and unknowingly continue healing. The healing was amplified by addressing the wounds through words. I am grateful for each *failed* attempt.

Interestingly enough throughout my suffering the creative flow intensified. I wrote approximately 100 songs over the span of four years, running the gamut from misery to elation. After worshiping my heroes and pain through melody I wrote *This Song We Sing*, a 10 song CD of empowerment, peace, gratitude, and stillness.

The final version of this book that you hold was written through neutral observation of my mind, or we may also say through a state of non-attachment. I was not uncomfortable writing and sharing because my past had been energetically resolved.

Thank you to my dear brother Joshua for being an inspiration for me to share my experience through this book.

Let this story of my life today alleviate our suffering with AIDS. Let it reveal the *one* we are so that each person may feel connected to their source and not so alone. Let it reveal the peace that always exists. Let it bring self-understanding, self-knowing, ego un-knowing, and self-revolution. Let it empower, illumine, heal, and awaken those that are suffering with AIDS, *AIDS Consciousness*, death, fear, or any limitation in their lives.

Let this book simplify God: *The Love which embraces and of which we are integral,* and AIDS into digestible doses of enlightenment.

This is my first book addressing my suffering and freedom from AIDS, and there is much to come. This book introduces you to my life and explains in detail my history of suffering and how I awoke. It speaks in detail concerning missions and their limitations, the *Habit of Seeking*, creating our sacred space, simplifying our lives, metamorphism, allergies, toxicity, cancer, steps to beginning meditation and more.

Thank you God; sing, write, speak, teach, laugh, dance, heal, and *be* through me. Thy will be done. Our will be done; for we are here now.

Thank you Calvin, my feelings for you are beyond measure. Without your love, caring, understanding, and support I would not be here, or be who I am today. You are a *golden angel* who has dressed my wounds and that fills me with such elation that I can hardly breathe. Thank you also for reading the drafts of this book and insightfully indicating areas that needed simplification or clarification. I love you.

Thank you to my incredible family that has fully accepted and loved me no matter the situation. I am humbled.

Thank you to all my friends, those with whom I speak and those that have fallen away. You are all a part of who I am and I love you.

Introduction

Through the current understanding of the accepted medical establishment I am a man with *full-blown* AIDS (less than 50 t-cells) who is expected soon to die. But I know that I am more than what they test for. I am.

This book is not only aimed at physically healing AIDS. We are healing our consciousness. It is through intake-awareness, nutrition, meditation, and other topics covered that we are addressing AIDS and our life experience holistically. This is the first book sharing my *cure* for the misperceptions that are creating AIDS and suffering in our lives. And so through my journey let us experience more of the *love* that we are; and in doing so we will heal.

Today let us not only be attached to the physical body because the body will do what the body does. We only need to *step* out of the way to know the oneness we are and all of our processes will harmonize. When we try to predict what our multi-dimensional body will do we suffer. So through being in a state of observation we then free the body to *be* and it balances.

This book explains that when we heal our consciousness it is then that we heal AIDS and our lives.

Let me reiterate concerning the physical that I was hospitalized in 2007 with double-pneumonia. I was told that I would not survive the infection but I was out of the hospital in only a few days. During my stay in the hospital I was consciously free and so the healing flowed. I observed as an expanded awareness throughout because my consciousness had been *healed*.

Here I am now sharing this book and living the truth that we are *more* than the body. We are more than dis-ease.

Let these words bring the realization that we are also more than any*thing* including sexuality and gender. We are pure awareness observing the body experience and we are eternally free and unscathed.

This book is not the Gospel. This is my unique journey and perspective and so please address your heart as you read.

This book is not an autobiography of my life. It begins in 1987 when AIDS entered my reality.

Contents

There is no-thing to seek.

you are that you are that you are that you are that you are that you are that you are that you are that

Let this book be as birds soaring

beyond the edge of storm

guiding us to ONE with their song.

Part 1

Those that survive

become a path of safe travel.

Preface

When AIDS enters our reality we are actually without realizing at a point in our life that is immeasurable in its potential for revolution. We may either succumb to the overwhelming energy of suffering from AIDS or through the slightest shift of our perspective be propelled up and out of all our suffering.

We have been pushed to such an extreme by AIDS physically, emotionally, and spiritually that we will either break through the bottom of the *trampoline* of life or be sent skyward at such a rate that we will reach heights unimagined. We will realize the peace and harmony conveyed and lived by those of saints, mystics, and many common a layperson. And this awareness is not exclusive it is available part and parcel to us all and I am now here to help us realize this.

I am here to show the world that AIDS does not need to be the end but it can and *is* the most fantastic and awe-inspiring opportunity to fully realize one's self.

We are more than AIDS and I am here now being more.

There are no *things* to fear, including our *death* for human beings are limitless. And through the journey of

my life let us transcend our fears and realize this freedom together.

Note: This book is *not* a book about finding a cure for AIDS. It is a book about *being* the cure through the realization that we are *more* than AIDS or any dis-ease.

Love

Let AIDS be known as *AIDS Consciousness*

Let me interject an understanding from here on out concerning AIDS and disease that will bring new depth and clarity. From this moment on let us know AIDS as *AIDS Consciousness,* and not only AIDS.

That at the core of a human being is a whole, vibrant, healthy, and limitless oneness to discover. *AIDS Consciousness* is disharmony to this experience. *AIDS consciousness* is the seed of an energetic weed that has grown and flourished untamed within our mind. It then infiltrates and affects so many of our mental processes that our *oneness* is *veiled* like leaves blocking the sun from reaching the floor of a forest.

So when we address, understand, and through unbiased observation of our lives absolve the *AIDS Consciousness* seed, the disharmony harmonizes. And our mind is now free to be the clear creative tool that *Love* has provided.

Be

1

Welcome to this Journey

Let me start off by proclaiming that I have been there and how. I have walked the AIDS walk and so now I am able share from within AIDS and from *beyond* AIDS. I am not a doctor and I do not have a college degree, though I did become a *Certified Holistic Health Consultant* in 2006. But what I bring is my *degree* is in my direct life experience of overcoming AIDS. So what I now offer is a palpable and direct message: we are more than AIDS or any dis-ease.

Some will attempt to explain what burning in a fire feels like through poetry, prose, or music, and this does heal on many levels. Or some will learn, assimilate, and share wisdom through parables, allegory, Koans, (eastern paradox poems) and more about the fire, the pain, and the suffering of life and this also has tremendous effect. But realize that I have physically and experientially sat and burned in a fire of such suffering through AIDS Consciousness that only the minutest spark of my life remained.

I have burned. I have suffered intolerably, and for years on end. I have been all-but destroyed to then become the proverbial *Phoenix* arising from the ashes of my life. Realize that I have not only experienced AIDS and dis-ease emotionally but also physically. I have lost lovers and friends in my life to AIDS. And I even eventually lost myself to AIDS to then one day suddenly awaken and discover who I truly am.

Let me now step into your shoes, center you, and offer you my strength and insights and you can then walk out of any nightmare of dis-ease or limitation and into a life of freedom.

Know that I have begged for death as I lay crumpled on the floor emptied of tears, crippled by countless fears, overwhelmed by the years, passing out from immeasurable pain, madness, and exhaustion to then awaken realizing our oneness. I have experienced so many relentless storms that suffering was all that I knew and lived for half of my life. Now, here in my 41st winter I am sharing my experience so that those suffering may realize peace, wholeness, and the freedom that we are. The freedom that is always available, and which AIDS and suffering illumined to me.

Let us open our mind and heart as we read and experience this book together. This book may bring smiles, gasps, confusion, tears, debate, expansion, and possible illumination and SELF-revelation.

This book will take us from my contracted consciousness of suffering and into larger and more expanded dimensions of love. We will travel *behind the scenes* of life through applications of awareness that pave the way to eternity. This book is multi-layered and multi-dimensional and it will benefit to read slowly.

May this book be all that it is at this time when so many here are suffering and leaving this planet due to their limited beliefs and understandings concerning AIDS, dis-ease, death, and limitation. When with this knowledge they may awaken to realize the inexpressible joy of *being*.

Love

2

My Life with AIDS

I was officially diagnosed HIV+ in 1994 during the last months of my third husband's life.

Moving forward, it was now 1995 and I had lost three dear and dedicated life partners and my best friend to AIDS in just over the span of eight years and I was exhausted, raw, and drained. It literally felt that I had been hit by a speeding truck. I was back living at home (again) with my loving and accepting parent's seeing that I had rejected the willed monies from my third lover so as not to deal with a lawsuit from acerbic and closed-minded in-laws. I did not have the energy or desire to *fight* for the money so I signed over of an amount that would have supported me for decades. At this time I had very few things and all of my belongings fit into my car.

When my first husband died in 1989 I lost our home. I could not afford the mortgage so I retained what little things I had and moved back into my childhood home. My first husband willed me a lot of money that I subsequently blew. A few months after his passing my sister and I rented an apartment together and I lived off of the money. Over the next few years I did not have any financial guidance and so I was more than happy to buy myself and my friend's gifts. I also paid most of the rent for our apartment. I bought an over-priced sports car and after about two years the money was gone.

After my second husband passed in 1992, three years after my first husband, I lost everything I owned. We were living in and renting a house from his parents and on the day he died they changed the locks on the doors and emptied out the house. I was again homeless and moved back in with my family. There was no will.

When my third husband passed in 1995 I lost my home for a third time, 95% of my things, my lover (again), and was living in my parent's spare bedroom trying to die.

I vividly recall lying in bed with the curtains drawn and praying to God, "Please let me die God. I can't take any more." I stayed in that bedroom for about two weeks depressed until one day I wondered if it was sunny outside beyond the closed curtains. So I got up, opened the curtains of the room and the window of my soul and continued on.

It was now 1995 and I was 27 years old with youth on my side so I was physically managing but spiritually I was

spent. I was deeply depressed and over life. I was directionless and disconnected and lost in my suffering.

Let me pause here and thank God for my incredible family. My mother, father, sister, and brother have always accepted me graciously and lovingly upon each return home. My family has always fully accepted me and I can never convey all that they mean and are to me. They embraced each lover as a family member and supported me throughout my journey and for this I am grateful.

So after my third husband passed and while I was living with my parents I was numb. I had experienced a nervous-breakdown during my third husband's dying months and its affect on me was powerful. Let me explain.

In 1994 while I was still living with my third husband I was in our bathroom entering our shower when my *breakdown* occurred. We had just returned home from a vacation upon where my life had been threatened. Someone had pulled a knife on me and told me that they were going to kill me because I was gay, and they meant it. This was it. I was energetically overloaded. Too much had already happened before this marriage that I had not resolved and my body just could not handle the stress or the amount of compounding energies. And so as I stood naked in our bathroom stepping into the water I removed my watch so as not to ruin it and time stopped. Literally

the scene froze. I realized that I had dropped my watch and it was still falling. My life was falling. I was falling.

I watched my watch fall for what seemed like minutes. And when the watch hit the tile floor and shattered I shattered along with it. My entire body began to itch. Every part of my skin was itching and I was overwhelmed. I was helpless. I ran screaming into the bedroom and flung myself onto the bed, writhing and rubbing against the sheets. My husband was in the same bed receiving IV's, and oh what a sight we must have been.

Imagine having an itch on a part of your arm and it really itches but that you cannot scratch it. This discomfort alone is enough to bother anyone, and unresolved may even drive someone mad. Now imagine that your entire body is itching. I mean your *entire* body itches and that you cannot do anything about it. You can scratch the skin but you still itch, and as you itch you only make it worse. This is how it was and it lasted all night. I itched for more than 6 hours straight. My body also physically shook throughout and my guilt did not help. I felt guilty that I was adding more stress on my dying husband by exposing him to my *drama,* and I hated this. I kept telling him that I was sorry as I shook wildly on the bed. My itching was upsetting him *and* our bed and what a trip it was. Thank God that a good friend of ours was a nurse and he answered our call and soon arrived with some pills. I don't remember what type of pills they were but I think that they were a muscle relaxant. I ended up taking about eight pills before I stopped itching and shaking. Amazingly, despite the pills I still did not fall asleep for a few days.

After my third husband's death I was living with my parent's and moving forward on my journey, but again I was dazed. And this nervous-breakdown also seemed to have erased much of my memory. It severely affected my thinking process (or my consciousness) and I later realized that this was one of the many blessings that I had received in disguise.

Praise God for the energetic overload and burnout which omitted the most painful situations and memories.

Now, this memory loss was not the type of memory loss where you have forgotten a certain day from a family vacation, oh no. This was like looking into your mind and only seeing huge walls of blackness with tiny threads of years (or of memories) in-between the monolithic ebony panels. When I tried to remember a scene during those intense and horrible times I could not. My memory was broken. I was broken. My inner-vision was fragmented and there were lengthy sections of time that were just, just gone. This mysterious *burnout* did keep me sane but it also removed any sense of continuity from my life. I was just sort of there on autopilot. I was present but I had no cognition to realize that I was present.

After my third husband passed I could not function, and driving a car was nearly impossible. I am sure I should not have driven but I did. And though I feared I was going crazy I was not going to give in to my insanity. I had gone to see a psychologist during the last quarter of my third husband's life per his wishes and she realized immediately the seriousness of my stress. My third husband was extremely worried about me and he knew about my history and so I agreed to go see the psychologist. But because of all of the suffering that I had been through when I shared my life story I was basically a black hole of misery engulfing the listener. This was heavy stuff that I was sharing and my friends and family of course did not know what to say.

During my first therapy session my therapist actually cried. I just sat there thinking, "This is hopeless. I will probably never heal. I can't believe I made my therapist cry." She felt so sorry for me, but I was feeling guilty that I was upsetting her so I could not relax. I went for one more session and realized that I did not have time for therapy. I needed to be the soldier because I was still in *battle.* It was like trying to cover an open wound with one hand while being stabbed as bullets reined in. This was war.

I also realized that a few weeks of therapy were not going to *fix* or heal me. I had serious issues. I was scared.

Be

3

The Insanity of it All

In 1995 after my third husband's death my mind was literally destroyed. After the energy-overload of all the years I could not coherently group more than a few thoughts together. Not many realized what I was going through. Because how can you tell your mom that you are deeply and disturbingly broken, depressed, and maybe even insane, *really* insane? How does Richie, the vibrant and creative brother say, "I am lost, and I really don't know what to do?" Actually I was too fractured to even define myself then and so I instinctually forged ahead.

Speaking was difficult. When I reached for a word to say it was clouded and in disarray. And so I chose not to speak at all and the ease of not speaking and slipping into the darkness was alarming. When I spoke it was as though I had to first rearrange the letters into a word. Then I needed to arrange these words into sentences and create a logical sentence flow and this was exhausting and

maddening. All that had been *normal* and easy was now a chore.

I remember a day that frightened me concerning my growing madness. After my third husband had died I was in a *Burger King* ordering a double cheeseburger when I lost my mind. I thought I was reaching into my pocket to grab my wallet but instead pulled my pants down as if I were going to use the bathroom. I was shocked. I could not fathom that I had almost exposed myself in a crowded line. I was dismayed. I felt crazy. I could not organize my thoughts and so I turned and ran out of the building and sat in my truck and cried for a long time.

There are many more scattered and shattered moments that I could share that could fill another book's pages. But the reason I am sharing this is because I am trying to convey the level of despair I felt and the condition of my consciousness after so many years of suffering and loss. And this suffering does not include my own experiential and immeasurable suffering with AIDS that begins years later. Let's just say that concerning varied and multi-dimensional suffering I have had my share.

Love

4

Losing Three Lovers

It is difficult for one to imagine the extreme heartache experienced with losing 3 lovers, husbands, wives, when losing one lover seems more than the heart can handle.

I lost three husbands to AIDS in nine years.

Each relationship with these beautiful and sensitive souls was over two years in length and so we *were* dedicated and energetically entwined. Each lover died horrifically. There was no peace in our lives because we were fighting for our survival in a sea of confusion and anger. Death is not easy for anyone and concerning AIDS there is not even a foundation of understanding for why what is happening *is* happening. Each of these men became sick after we met and I remained with them until they left this world.

My first husband was an early case of AIDS in Orlando. He went from vibrant and peaceful man to misery and death in less than two years. When we met he was HIV+

yet healthy. He started taking the medications for AIDS and within less than a year on the medications he became sick and passed. He took five pills of AZT every few hours and I intuitively knew that this was too much toxicity for his body. He suffered so.

My second husband had a history of drug abuse, depression, anger, and he also shared many dark secrets with me on his death bed concerning his past that supported AIDS or *AIDS Consciousness.* His battle was intense. He was combative, violent, and angry. He hit and abused me throughout our relationship and during his final months he experienced dementia and the loss of body functions. I was his caretaker though he had lost the ability to communicate and had forgotten who I was. Those were heavy and painful times.

When I met my third husband he was HIV+ and taking the *Cocktail,* the standard prescribed medications for AIDS. He declined quickly in the span of two years. This man was a powerhouse of selfless-service, love, and creativity. He was an angel. He too was crushed by AIDS, or we can now say by the toxic medications he took.

Concerning what causes AIDS, or *AIDS Consciousness* we will acquire this understanding together throughout this voyage. I will say that what is prescribed today for AIDS is less in strength than what was prescribed in the early 90's, though what is prescribed today it is still

incredibly powerful and toxic to the body. I feel that the *Cocktail* prescribed for these men was too much for their bodies to process and their bodies simply broke down.

Let us now open our minds and hearts to the possibility that there is more to AIDS than just a *virus*. Let us realize that there are more factors to take into consideration when discussing AIDS or dis-ease.

Be mindful of the incredibly powerful and toxic medications that are prescribed for HIV and AIDS.

Be

5

Gay and Straight, My Dual Existence

Words do not approach or point to the state that I was in. I felt such misery, anger, and confusion at life that it just floored me. I was angry, so angry because I did not understand anything that was going on. How could God take away these three men that I loved, and through such torture?

To further explain the fracture of my psyche I was also during these deaths the lead-singer in a *straight* band. I was living straight *and* gay. Let me explain.

During the suffering and passing of my first two husbands I was not *out* to my friends. I was in the closet. On one hand I was the lead-singer in local bands perceived as a *straight* man and on the other I was a gay man living with my lovers. It was maddening. I was two *completely* different people. In one life I was 20-something and straight. I partied and even *dated* (or talked and led on) girls. I told consistent and creative lies and actually

everything was a lie and I felt so guilty. I was trapped and I hated the situation that I was in.

So I hung out with my band-mates, truly being one of them on all levels even though I was miserable inside. And what was heavy is that when I was with them I became so good at *acting* straight that I would forget who I really was until I was in my car driving to see a dying lover in the hospital. I would be in the hospital at one moment supporting a lover and then on stage in another performing as the *straight* lead singer. And this constant mental shifting was insanity.

I remember one time during my first husband's passing when I was at a band practice and on the verge of losing it. And this was only the first death of a lover and I was already overwhelmed and stressed.

On a side note, I realize that many have lived a life of lies when they were *coming out*, and that this seems *par for the course*. Some may have even lost a lover or friends to AIDS and my heart goes out to them. And if this would have been all that I experienced my life would not be what it is. But it was the non-stop loss and chaos following and during the deaths of my husband's that slowed my healing and magnified my lunacy. However, this journey did eventually bring realization and my revolution and so I am grateful.

So here I was only 21 years old and going mad. I had just left the hospital room of my dying first husband (he had double pneumonia, of which he did not survive) and was now sitting in band practice fuming and about to explode.

I did not have anyone to share my suffering with. I could not share what I was going through with my band mates because these were 19 year old boys mostly thinking about music and girls and not aware of AIDS. They were boys still living at home; and I may have only been two years older but it felt like 20. You see I was their *straight* and eccentric lead singer yet unbeknownst to them I was already living on my own, gay, and my husband was in the hospital dying of AIDS.

I would sit and look at my wedding ring (I had told them that it was my dad's ring) during band practice in complete dismay at my life. I sat there disconnected somehow managing not to cry as we wrote silly pop songs, laughed, and ate pizza. Those were excruciating times.

Love

6

Being Beyond Sexuality

Let me pause the story now and interject concerning sexuality. After a deep immersion in stillness while meditating I realized that all of life is energy. This was not an intellectual understanding because I felt this. I was experiencing this. In meditation as I observed my mind I realized that I was being *beyond* what I thought myself to be because I was observing thoughts. I was beyond what I had understood myself to be. I was formless awareness, and there was no individual *me* in this awareness. This realization literally blew my mind. It took me some time to re-acclimate back into my life after experiencing this formlessness. Because when we are infinite awareness there is not even a mind, there is only a pure observing eternity.

And concerning sexuality and gender, as I observed my consciousness I realized that I was not only a man, a gay man, or any*thing* for that matter. I was the formless soil out of which these beliefs grew. And realizing this I

became free. So today let us release our limited notions of human sexuality and embrace that we are more than the body and more than our people stories. That we are here now opening to more of our *oneness* through the surrendering of concepts such as sexuality and gender.

Realize that at the *core* of what we experience as our life there is a pure awareness beyond all definition. We could also say that there is a form of formlessness that we now point towards with our words, including the word *energy.* But words are not *it*. And no emotional state is *it*. It is more. And sexuality and gender are not formless, so can we let our attachments to sexuality and gender go and now transcend into more? Can we now just flow as one awareness without the need to label ourselves?

Human being consciousness springs forth up and out of pure awareness and we are now who we think we are; an evolving transcending consciousness. Let me state a very simple observation that may free us all of our ancient and powerful energetic limitations.

There is no sexuality in awareness. Awareness is whole because it contains everything.

If we think in terms of masculine and feminine energy we transcend the physical body and the limitations that we have placed upon it.

Realize that gender is *created* here as organization and procreation for these bodies. But we are more than the body. And again there is no wrong or right to our life experience as this is the way it is. We are here grateful to experience this miraculous journey. And when we continually release the definitions that we have of ourselves (including definitions of sexuality and gender) we disentangle the mind and we further expand into the *one* that we are.

We cannot deny that concerning our physical bodies there are fundamental differences. There *is* sexuality here on Earth. But we know this and have known this and so now can we transcend this limited idea of physicality to know the awareness of which we are integral?

We are more than sexuality.

We are more than male, female, heterosexual, homosexual, or any of the other gradients of human experience. And we are also more than being a man or woman because these are also vibratory creations within this Earth consciousness. The human body is basically created by the earth environment to *house* our awareness. We have *entered* and morphed into life to be here. And because of this we require a certain *life-suit* to experience creation because we are *more* than creation.

I do not claim to understand the why or the how of our arriving here. What I am pointing to is the unlimited truth that we always *are* in any created environment. I do not point to the details of dimensions because there are many now proficient in this regard. What I do offer is a light that illumines the awareness that we all are in any situation or circumstance. And this light is now shining upon the concepts of sexuality and gender. And this light is the same light that freed me of my attachment to sexuality and gender consciousness.

OK; let's get back to the story.

I watched my three husbands fight valiantly for their lives, though unsuccessfully. They each strictly adhered to the advice of their allopathic doctor and followed the current beliefs concerning AIDS. I observed each man struggle with every ounce of energy to live only to eventually in vain succumb to AIDS. I will say that during these times a larger part of me was observing my life from an expanded state. And that I drew countless times from those horrible and yet oh so enlightening experiences as I came to my own SELF-understanding journeying in, out, and beyond my suffering.

Each step we need to cherish; for it has taken each step to bring us to where we are.

During the nine years of losing my husband's I was many people, or we could also say many personalities. I was a husband, a friend, and a caretaker. Let me share that in the beginning of each marriage our life was wonderful, new, and without drama. However, just when everything was flowing and I was starting to heal AIDS arrived, and with a vengeance. Just when I thought AIDS was finally out of my life and I could truly relax and heal here was AIDS again. All that I knew was AIDS.

During these lives I changed hundreds of adult diapers and changed countless soiled sheets. I wiped away streaming tears and streaming blood. I comforted and cradled dying souls and barely slept. I felt like a soldier at the frontline of battle who was being continually caked in the blood and mud of the exploding moments. Bombs went off hourly. Life was chaos. I was young, naïve, and yet clueless, but this was my situation and I did what needed to be done to the best of my ability.

To note, I have always been compassionate and hyper-aware of another's feelings. And I find great joy in talking with someone and helping them feel better. And so helping someone in distress and illness did not seem that inappropriate. So I took these situations on with a feeling of thankfulness that I could be there for these dying and suffering men during the hardest parts of their journey here on earth. Something within me was immense and capable, and it provided me with the energy and strength that I needed no matter what the situation. I never once entertained the idea of abandoning them.

I was there. I was a soldier.

I was grateful and I also *thought* that this was my mission.

Be

7

Transcending My Mission

Let me share a powerful insight concerning *missions*. Missions are illusions in that missions are mind-based attachments that only lead into more mind. And when I realized this I transcended my mission. This mission belief was a belief that had governed my life up until I was in my late 30's. I was so securely attached to and controlled by the idea of having a mission that I was not free to be. I was always on some mission, but for what, and for whom?

I feel now is a good time to introduce missions and the limitation of having a mission consciousness. This *mission* transcendence is analogous to a key that opens a large door which then reveals more small locked drawers. It is a way to we travel deeper *into* our mind.

The mission belief was always there penetrating and comingling with my consciousness that all of my experience was somehow apart of a mission. How many times have we been made aware that we have a *mission*?

We think that there is some mysterious *thing* that we must do to satisfy God? And unless we achieve this certain mission sometime or somewhere that we are not living correctly, or that we are sinning, too many.

Do you see the limitation inherent in this thinking? Do you see the stress that is amplified when one is suffering or near death? A person will be haunted by the fact that they don't have time to complete the mysterious mission. And we realize that they could do anything and still not be in joy because they are always comparing their experience to the *mythical* mission. This is a limiting belief that needs to be transcended to realize peace. And concerning AIDS, (or AIDS Consciousness), surrendering the mission is a powerful step towards SELF-realization.

I had an interesting conversation with an acquaintance. It is incredible experiencing another aspect of the mystery of creation in a person and what the mystery reveals when neutrally observing. As we were sharing we each began to speak candidly about the inner-experiences we each have had. I know this tends to lead to inexplicable areas of conversation but nevertheless we continued sharing. During our conversation they stated the word *mission* enough time for me to notice. And as we continued I became more aware of this *mission-consciousness* they were living. And through observing their *mission consciousness* I was inspired to examine my own.

"A mission" I thought. "What exactly is a mission? And who am I trying to satisfy anyway?" This person I was sharing with was formulating larger and larger conceptual projects, some possibly even global, and this certain point I now make. This individual was on a *mission*, and so conclusively that the direction, future, and the eventual projects themselves were all under this *mission-umbrella*. "A mission" I asked, "What does this mean to you?" And so they shared their inspiration and what God tells them to do and it was beautiful, but it did not *feel* free and flowing, it felt limited. It felt like they were riding on a train upon which they could dance, laugh, sing, design, build, teach, heal, suffer, or do whatever but they were still on the train. They were on a train of a mission of which they did not realize. And so I tried not to judge them or the situation but something felt limited.

I started to wonder what it means when we say "I have a mission." This conversation and the reminding of a mission sent me deep into my own mind and into my belief about a mission. Realize that we are each a mirror revealing the other to themselves. I realized that having a mission is experiencing a mind that first needs to *fix* things to then know peace. And I can see this continuing today in the new *spiritual* business paradigm. I can also recognize this within layers of new *and* old teachings. What they are saying is "Let us *fix* you *for* you." And so how will a person ever find wholeness if they only look to separate *things* for

their wholeness? How will they know peace if they are only seeking out what they *think* needs fixing? Because this is illusion because they are only fixing what they currently believe is broken. But this changes constantly. They will end up seeking and *fixing* things forever trying to be become happy, not realizing the wholeness that always IS. There is no*thing* to *fix* in wholeness. And in order to fulfill a *mission* a person would also need to experience a reality that requires solving or *fixing*. They would need to have a hunger (or a desire) to justify the mission. And I thought "Where is peace in this equation? Where is our gratitude for our life? Where is the acceptance of the greater unknown? Where is non-judgment of our total experience?" I also deeply wondered, "How could this ever resolve?"

I realized that you could be in an impoverished slum or in some other heavenly realm of evolved existence and you would still see what you *think* needs fixing. And ultimately you would be deep in the stories of the mind and not experiencing the harmony (or wholeness [or holiness]) of the space that you are in. So I have realized that I do not want or have a mission. I also realized that having a mission was a large part of my limited belief-consciousness that was draining me. I had created a mission to save the world. And until the world was *saved*, I would be on that mission indefinitely. I realize that I came into life thinking that I needed to save everyone and everything. But this was an immature observation. What I really needed to do was to know myself. Observing my mission freed me of missions and illumined the present moment to me. It returned the energy that was sustaining the mission and I realized more than having a mission. I was now free to flow.

Let us now transcend our missions by opening to the possibility that missions are limiting our life experience. Because when we worry about what we should do tomorrow the opportunity that is before us is then missed. When we look at our greater *teacher* in action we see that despite what we *think* or feel needs *fixing* all is balanced. All is in harmony. Nature is not unbalanced our perception of nature is. And the further we step back to observe nature the clearer that nature's design becomes. *Nature will add and remove and we only need to observe in awe.* What we today are experiencing in nature as *wrong* is the result of experiments attempted through our growing understanding of nature. There is no *right* or *wrong*, only expanded patterns to recognize. So through wisdom can we let it all be just as it is? Can we let nature take care of itself and now take care of ourselves?

We can construe the shifting tectonic plates as a horrible result of sinful actions or we can move beyond this limited thinking and know that life is impermanence.

When we observe without conceptual attachment we are at peace no matter the situation.

Let us ask now ourselves "Is life chaos, or is what we are experiencing just the natural ephemeral expression of nature not to be feared?" Meditate on this for more clarity.

8

Transcending the Habit of Seeking

Let us address another aspect of our consciousness as we discuss the limitation of missions that when transcended opens a life in joy. Let us now discuss the *Habit of seeking*.

As I began consciously *awakening* I still found myself on occasion looking into a new teaching or spiritual belief and this baffled me. I was quickly absorbing and absolving this new information but I wondered what is it that is causing me to seek? I began to examine my mind to discover what was pulling me out of my center. I had expanded from the limitations that had usually *caught* my attention, though not always smoothly. And I was now a wider and freer awareness, so what was I still looking for? And why was I turning away from myself for the answers? What structure existed in my consciousness that was used to seeking externally for the answers? I realize that something within would feel incomplete and send me out seeking until I would again realize that I did not need any*thing* for wholeness. I was thinking that I would find completeness through an external teaching and so I continued to habitually seek. But through the limited *feeling* of the external teaching I would realize that I did not need the teaching to be whole. And amazingly I began to recognize a limitation still in my consciousness: a *habit of seeking*. I knew that when I was not thinking that I was stillness and that stillness is without individual vibration so stillness *is* wholeness.

And so when I recognized that I was habitually seeking for the truth I stopped and sat in *Love*. And the impetus (or the seeking habit) that had sent me *out* for truth was now realized as the limited belief that it was. I stopped seeking and I knew.

As the *Habit of Seeking* dissolved, the amount of time that I spent passing through a belief lessened proportionately as my awareness grew, or we could also say as my awareness deepened. The way I can explain this is that after being *in* a new teaching I started to feel confined by the teaching. And seeing that I was able to observe the confined feeling I was then free of that confinement. We do not realize that we are confined until we are aware enough to observe the entire situation, like knowing the forest by understanding the collective trees of the forest. I realized that I did not need to acquire a

new external belief for wholeness. Being aware is wholeness.

When I visited a new teaching that did not know its own completeness I became uncomfortable as I tried to conform to the new teaching. This understanding has matured in that when we realize our wholeness we can walk anywhere in the world and be at peace. We know who we are; though for me it took more SELF-understanding to get this is space of peace.

It is as though I needed to pretend that I was incomplete for me to feel comfortable with other seekers. Though I tasted wholeness I still desired a spiritual community for resonant understanding. And I realize that this desire to belong was actually a part of the dissolving habit of my seeking. Now I do not need *spiritual* because all relationships are valuable and illuminating.

Interestingly enough, this understanding of seeking also revealed to me that my existing relationships were more than I had thought them to be. I realized that all relationships are holy and it only our beliefs and judgments that obscure this. The deeply engrained belief that was stating that I needed to up and leave my life to go do some*thing* more *enlightened* was an immature understanding. It was a part of the mission. And once I surrendered the mission and seeking I was free.

It is interesting to observe that because we have been seeking ourselves for so long the seeking itself becomes a habit, and a powerful core habit at that. And there comes a certain point when we need to address this habit so we realize a life of more than seeking. I found myself seeking out of deep habit even when in my heart I knew wholeness. This is a multi-dimensionality that is not easily explained because as we are awakening we are conscious as the observer and also as the merging limited idea that we had of ourselves.

There was a *stage* in my growing understanding when I was basically afraid to be whole. I knew who I was but I was still energetically disassociating from my past habits, and the emptiness I felt was staggering. I was in a conundrum. I was still in-between the two poles of my seeking and my knowing. This resembling a person slowly turning away from one sun, the sun of ego, to feeling another sun, the sun of wholeness. And at a certain point both suns are within the peripheral inner vision and we are torn. We are aware of the old understanding and the new understanding simultaneously. And we are being pulled energetically in different directions. The *pull* back to our limitation is weak compared to the pull into our wholeness. But the pull back towards the ego may be amplified when a limited resonation in our consciousness occurs, such as a core fear.

I knew who I was, but the individual consciousness I *thought* I was still energetically existed. Energy transmutes and cannot be created or destroyed so the energy of ego was not ending, it was only returning to the sea of formlessness. And even though the limited idea of me (or my ego) had mostly been assimilated back into wholeness it was still giving its final tug at my mind and so I continued seeking. This ego was now a mere whisper in a trumpet of knowing. And at times we must strain to discern the between the voice of the ego and the knowing of the one. There was an acclimation process of a few years as the *habit of seeking* concluded breaking down returning to the *energy sea of love potentials. There is a reason and need for every experience; observe life neutrally until all experiences become love.*

So I was being affected by the remaining, detaching, and returning energies of the old gargantuan *habit of seeking*. I was balancing, and yet some habits were still running up until the last thread of their dissipating energy. There is a logical explanation as to how and why we are consciously evolving, or why we are *spiraling* into *oneness.* There is a *reason* that we don't instantly realize our *oneness.* There is a reason we gradually step-by-step realize who we are, and this next chapter attempts to simplify and encapsulate this: *The Gradient of Becoming*. This chapter may seem out of place, but it helps to expand the mind and the heart as we deepen into this journey.

Be

9

The Gradient of Becoming

Why do we Spiral into *oneness*? Let us together examine this occurrence of *spiraling* and the reason that it occurs as a spiral.

Imagine you are standing holding a candle in a room. Envision the room being illumined by this single candle and think of this candle also as your current *level* of awareness. Now imagine that your current *level* of understanding expands out as far as the single candle illumines. Your life is illumined by the light of the candle.

Now let us imagine being in this same room but there are now 1,000,000 lamps shining brightly. What would we now *see?* What reality would be experienced? All would be light. You would only see bright light. You could not look out and see the furniture, the walls, or even yourself. When you reached to feel yourself you would only *feel* light. You would only know one light. Light would *be*. This light would engulf you and so your body would be light.

This is why certain *spiritual* teachings state (to the effect of) "No man shall stand before our God." This is not based on Dogma or on karma. This is also not a fear-based, rule it is just physics. If we *stood* before God (or in the light of wholeness), the ego that we daily experience would be assimilated into the 1,000,000 lamps of God, so to speak. We would not know any*thing* but light. The single candlelight ego would be absorbed by the 1,000,000 lamplight of *love* and there would only be one.

As we spiral out we are hypothetically, and one-by-one, turning on a new *lamp* of understanding. Each lamp then further illumines more of our *oneness* to us, and each step also unifies our ego with the one and illumines the limitations to us that were in the shadow of our mind. We are essentially *soul-acclimating* to each new lamp of understanding that we experience so as to remain at our current *individual* level of awareness. We are learning the light that we *are* while maintaining who we think we are at each new step of our conscious expansion.

This acclimation is similar to when we exit a store and step into the bright sun where we need a moment or two for our eyes to dilate to the light. And the time it takes for dilation is proportionate to how varying the two sources of light are. When we are exiting a well-lit store and stepping into the bright sun the change is not that drastic, and so we only require a few seconds for re-acclimation. But,

when we are say exiting a dark cave, or we may also say exiting years of our depression, when we step into the bright sun the change may be explosive, and even painful. We then instantly shield our eyes from the sun, or we may even say we hide our ego from God. This spiraling acclimation is what's occurring at the soul-level of our experience. We are step-by-step through our awareness opening (or walking into) brighter and brighter suns of *oneness* to remain aware throughout the expansion.

We could not plug an *I-pod* directly into a power-station lest it would be destroyed right, this is elementary. So we need to plug the I-pod directly into an energy source that is only one fraction of the energy of the entire power station for it to operate.

Because if an ego shifted instantly into wholeness, it would disappear, and so would all semblance that the previous identity. And this would be too much to handle. And so step by step we discover who we truly are.

We spiral up in our consciousness.

Love

10

Realizing Gratitude through Nature

Now that we have more understanding towards spiraling consciousness and the *habit of seeking* let us deepen a little more into missions.

When we take for example a person living on earth with a mission could we say that the Earth can cater to this person and all of their needs because they are here? Yes. Then can we also say that when taking into account an Indian sage, or a new age teacher, or one who whom we consider to be *awake* that the Earth provides for them equally as well? Yes. So the Earth supports everyone right, but how is this possible? Is it not then that the experience is in the eye of the beholder? Yes. Do we not realize that we only see want to see to satisfy our current level of understanding? Yes. Can we then state that not one of these realities has precedence over another reality, just as one tree or animal species does not have precedence over the other? Sure. All is now in balance.

Nature knows what it is doing.

When we accept that all *things* belong we may then accept the Earth. And we will experience peace by not trying to *fix* things but through observing, evolving, and expanding into our own harmony.

Imagine what we will experience when we allow the unbridled moment to flow through us. What if we surrender our limited beliefs?

A belief is an understanding that is based upon one's existing store of information. But realize that we don't need to believe in anything to be here now. The present moment is not created by yesterday or tomorrow, it is here now flowing.

Sit and ponder how much energy is being spent on the *not-now*. It is remarkable isn't it? Do you see how through living in our mind fantasies that we are not truly addressing the present source of our imbalance, we are only addressing our minds? That we are only rearranging the effects and symptoms of what was and what may be and we are not expanding? And that if we took the energy that is fueling our conservation efforts, animal preservation, global warming causes, or any *fix it* consciousness and invested it into new inspired companies that the lesser-evolved stagnant creations that are *disrupting* nature will starve and naturally fade away, as well as their affects? Realize that what we think are now problems will be *solved* through the sheer joy of life expressing itself. We only need to be present. We may address the global issues, yes, but if we want SELF-revolution we need to reverse the poles of what we deem important.

Let us create new ways of being and not new ways of healing.

If we want true change then let us unite now and *be* the change. The solutions we seek are not found in the *mistakes* of yesterday or in the dreams of tomorrow, they are realized through being aware. How can we clear the river-water around the corner from the unregulated factory that is dumping its waste into it? Or spend monies on creating safe environments for animals when it is the accepted and un-governed companies that are causing the environmental problems that are funding the conservation efforts in the first place? Do we see that this design may be bypassed by using our energy not to feed the ego but through unifying and being aware now?

We can see that nature does know what it is doing far more than we do at this moment so let nature do what it does. Then in our joy we will create new companies that create new harmonies because this is what they do, not because they are required to. Nature does not try and repair a bloom that has fallen to the earth, it grows a new bloom. And what is amazing is that nature still experiences life through the transmuting eternal energy of the fallen bloom. Nature experiences the journey through the elements that comprised the flower, fallen or not,

Ask yourself, "If nature only spent its energy on fixing things how could it create?"

Earth, Mother, Gaia, or in whatever way that you associate with our planet, is our teacher. The lessons expressed through nature are so numbered and diverse that we could never know them all in one lifetime or even in thousands of lifetimes so maybe we don't have to. Let us take this opportunity to awaken to the realization that all of life is balanced, and it is only our perspective that skews this understanding. One way for awakening is through our acceptance and gratitude for all that we experience through nature.

Be

11

Dimensions, Music, and Being

Life is continually asking us to surrender our attachments and expand our awareness, and through observing nature we can do this. Because when we accept the overall balance of nature we then realize the overall balance of our total experience. So is it not logical that through observing nature's balance we may now balance as a race of people? Yes. Can we also see that when we learn oneness through nature's example that we will also open up for new and unlimited experience? Yes. Could we also say that by seeing that the body is impermanent that we would continue to experience the earth as we know it through our energetic attachments after the body ceases until we surrender to our oneness? Let's find out. We can explore these questions through physics and the laws of nature that we understand at this time.

Today we accept that we are integrated in a field of intelligence that is beyond our comprehension. We also realize that everything is interconnected and interrelated. So concerning the earth we can say that it is our *conscious-*

interplay, or our energetic attachments to the earth that incorporate us into this octave of earth experience, or into this planetary existence. Let us realize that we are threads of an energetic light tapestry that are interwoven into the consciousness that is here in this dimension. OK; the architecture of what we ARE is vast and indefinable so let's approach this from another perspective. Let's approach this through a musical analogy.

When we are living a life of middle "C", and middle "C" is earth consciousness as we know it, then we can surmise that we are here as middle "C" consciousness. So if mission consciousness is also within this earth octave (earth consciousness being the note of middle "C" to the next "C") we may conclude that despite the transmuting impermanence of our energetic bodies that we will continue to be *born* on earth. We will energetically re-transmute as a human being seeing that earth is middle "C" and contains mission consciousness. Theoretically we are then in a self-perpetuating loop of the universe creating the limited situation that we have *asked* for. *Love* is satisfying our current evolutionary beliefs concerning missions until we through neutral observance we realize that our life is just truly the expression of joy, and not a mission-based *job*. We are then free to experience life without attachment because we realize that we are more than the threads. And we may now be free to experience any note within any musical octave of consciousness.

Our mission is to be, and "being" is more than a mission.

When we are *being*, or when we are aware of the love and wholeness that we are we may still do exactly what we were doing before in *mission-consciousness.* But we are now doing what we are doing from an expanded consciousness. We are not limited by our egos. We are not attached to missions and we are limitless.

We then express just for the joy of expressing. We sing to sing and express the arts through the joy of being aware. We create businesses because this is expressing who we are and the facets of business, organization, and growth bring us joy. We teach out of our joy of teaching, sharing and expanding as one together. We learn new knowledge realizing that we are only learning more of ourselves. We heal not because we think people *need* healing but because we love life and know all as one. We are life. We are love and we only see and know love so this is all that we do and all that we are.

It may seem like a small thing that I am pointing out here but this is beyond mere semantics and is a far-reaching shift.

Let this, the tiniest of shifts from *mission-consciousness* to freedom occur just by observing now that this shift may happen. Again, when we are observing the mission consciousness we are free of missions. We are metaphorically the ocean observing the waves. And so we only need to observe and remind ourselves daily until the *mission consciousness* fades and the energy returns to the quantum *sea of potentials.*

Another thing to realize is that when we are living within a confined consciousness we tend to express through a recycled means. And this is analogous to everyone on a plane inhaling and exhaling the same air until upon landing the door is opened and new air flows in. And so when we detach from missions, more than missions is realized and new inspiration *arrives.* We also could say that our experience is being expressed through confined and recycled means due to our limited beliefs. We have contracted into a smaller awareness and so we are not connecting to our full potential. We are only rearranging existing *things* and not flowing in the moment.

Conversely, if we neutrally observe our life and not attach ourselves to any beliefs, we are then naturally flowing through the octaves of our understanding. We are then not only a part of middle "C" consciousness, we are more. Now the newness (or the potentials) manifest through us while we are here physically. We have *opened* to the more that we are. We are now spirit in the flesh. We know *heaven* here on earth. We understand "as above so below" and so we enrich the Earth chord with new holy harmonics. We have joined the circle.

Interesting enough, if we aware of more than "C" consciousness then where are we and what are we, and also, what is being through us?

The only mission is to awaken.

Love

12

The Twists and Turns of Life

Let us now continue with my life history as these insights on missions, the habit of seeking, and the limitation of the ego, our multi-dimensional existence, and the role of nature are assimilated.

In these lives with my husband's we were living and we were playing together. We were basically just normal married couples with normal responsibilities. We were working separately or together, going on vacations, going out to clubs, taking trips to the beach, hanging out with our friend's, and just living life. However, we were also going to doctor's visits and battling mysterious illnesses while admitting lovers into hospitals not knowing if they would survive the stay.

I have no regular flow to my life for more than a decade only to then lose that *normal* flow when I myself become ill. But back to my history with my lovers, we will talk about my personal journey with AIDS in depth later in this book.

During the many hospital stays I slept in provided hospital chairs for so many days that I lost count. I lost all semblance of the passing of time. I had no idea what the month was or even the year. I realized that my hair was falling out by seeing the clumps of hair inside my baseball cap each time I removed it after a poor attempt to sleep in the hospital room. I gazed into the mirror to only see a stranger peering out at me. A person that had not slept for countless months and who was now reacting through instinct alone, wild-eyed with intense focus.

For my lovers I was a caring mother, a supportive father, a brother, a lover, a fighter, and also a nurse. I will say that every experience I experienced, be it one of joy or one of horror revealed a new piece of life to me, of which I now offer holistically.

Be

Part 2

My Experiential Suffering with AIDS

Love

13

Advanced HIV Disease

In 1994 while my third husband was still living I went to see an infectious disease doctor due to my lack of energy and the parade of minor illnesses I was experiencing, especially facial skin disorders. I also went because I was a gay man whose lover was now dying of AIDS. I had tested HIV negative up until that point but I was now afraid. I also was not always what was considered *safe* with my third husband while cleaning him or when changing his IV's and so this was weighing on my mind as well. There were many emergencies when I did not have the time to stop and put on a pair of gloves, and so I didn't.

Let me say that there is still to this day *no* conclusive evidence concerning the relationship between HIV and AIDS, and there is a reason for this that is found in the silence of the heart. Because AIDS is not contagious it is a severely compromised immune system. Remember that empirical information is to be transcended to find eternal freedom from AIDS and our suffering. Be mindful of mental attachments. Listen to your body.

So in 1994 I discovered that I had 444 T-Cells. I was incredibly stressed after my suffering and losses so having a low t-cell count should not have been unexpected. But this information about how the immune system may be suppressed in times of high stress was not shared with me. All that was shared was that I was now dying like my lover and those before him.

This doctor did not speak to me holistically. He did not ask me about my past experiences, if I was resting or how I was sleeping. This doctor also did not ask about my nutrition or if I was getting enough exercise. He did not ask if I was seeing a therapist or even how I was doing *spiritually*. All that he did and knew to do was to take blood, follow the standard allopathic protocols, and fill me with fear concerning HIV and AIDS propaganda in our dialogues. He also prescribed incredibly toxic medications. That is all. I was one in a long line of patients to him. I do know that he was overwhelmed and learning as well and this is fine because his bedside manner and limited consciousness illumined much for me as I reflected on my life during my own years of suffering.

My experience with doctors and disease inspired me to become a Holistic Health Consultant. Because all is a gift when we observe and experience without attachment, even situations that appear negative.

Continuing on, this doctor in Orlando was AIDS, AIDS, AIDS, like the majority in the 1980's and 1990's were.

I will interject that the latest doctor I *partnered* with here in Michigan, *Dr. B.,* was very understanding and empathetic to my plight. He did everything in his power to assist me even though he did not fully understand my *spiritual awakening*. He was not knowledgeable of my inner process of self-healing, or acceptant of my discontinuing of the AIDS medications. And this is OK, as we are all learning more of the oneness that we are in our own way.

There must be those that invite us into new expanded dimensions of consciousness else the current system would collapse. And *physics* clearly states that a closed energetic system will break down. When an energetic system stops receiving energy from the larger system it implodes.

Dr. B. has a heart of gold and I am blessed that he has been a part of my healing team.

Doctors only address part of the whole, and because of this, with them alone we will not wholly heal.

After my first consultation in 1994 where I learned of having only 444 t-cells I was haunted and worried due to the previous experiences with my lovers' deaths and my current lover's suffering. My t-cells were now low and my lover's t-cell counts were low and this was not good.

The medical establishment's emphasis on low t-cells, along with the media's propaganda concerning low t-cell counts was confusing to me. Two of my lovers had started the drugs for AIDS when they found out their t-cells were in the 400's and here I now was in the same predicament.

A year later in 1995 and I am watching my third husband fade horribly. We had been in and out of the hospital with pneumonias and mysterious ailments and we were exhausted. He was now a skeleton and barely alive. He was on too many medications and he was taking them like candy which I intuited were making him more ill.

A part of me realized that my lover was toxic. And so I questioned his doctor numerous times as to the real cause of his illness but did not accept his pat answers. I was researching myself into the medications they prescribe for AIDS and what I was finding out about these "drugs" was shocking, even scary. And each time I asked his doctor if he felt the medications may be too powerful, or if they could possibly damage his organs he flat out denied it. I did not like the feeling that his doctor was not even open to the possibility that these drugs were harmful. He felt emotionally closed off and in a psychological shell. And the more I researched into these drugs the more I realized the toxicity of what he was being prescribed. My lover's liver eventually failed. I was told that HIV had gathered and attacked and consumed his liver, but I never bought this answer.

These medications that I had found so much varying degrees of information and quite horrific insights into were the very same medications I was now expected to take for my illness – no thank you. I did not start any medications for advanced HIV Disease much to the chagrin of that doctor. He told me I would probably be dead in two or three years, and yet here I am.

It was 1995 and I was petrified. I thought about dying for the first time in my life, really dying, and this thought was not resolved until I *awoke.*

Concerning t-cell counts, a count of 450 t-cells is the lowest accepted count for *normal* t-cell levels. Abnormal counts begin below 450. The bottom range of normal, despite being in the normal range is considered *Advanced HIV Disease,* and this is where I now was.

Be

14

1996: Trapped and Depressed

It is now 1996 and a few years have passed. My third husband has died and I am now by the grace of God managing a *normal* life (again) despite the incredible losses I experienced and my current mental suffering. I am in the deepest love I have known with my husband Cal, (with whom I am still with today 13 years later), but I am also becoming more and more tired. I am suffering from painful facial dermatitis as well as experiencing large boils on my forehead. Not a great place to have boils in an image-conscious world.

There is no escape from the staring eyes when your face is chaffing and bright red. You are basically a walking billboard that states “I am not normal”. I felt that I was under constant surveillance. I felt like I was under a microscope and I just could not relax. If the night before I had experienced a facial breakout I dreaded going into work, and these breakouts happened weekly. I said countless times to Cal that I would rather have something internally wrong than to have to deal with a red, bleeding, and chaffing face.

It was very stressful to be reminded weekly by my coworkers that I appeared abnormal. They would ask, "Why is your face so red Rich?" or "What is wrong with you?" and I would then get self-conscious and struggle for an answer such as "I must have eaten something that I am allergic to." This allergy excuse became my normal answer for years and I was still lying and despised this.

In 1996 while experiencing this painful facial dermatitis, boils, allergies and heavy fatigue Cal and I have a heart-to-heart discussion and I agree to start taking the prescribed combination of powerful nuclear medications for a person with Advanced HIV Disease. I am stressed and I fear that I am slowly dying on Cal. And the last thing I wanted to do was to cause Cal or my family any more grief.

I would rather suffer the worst know suffering than to cause them pain and maybe I have.

Love

15

The "Cocktail" and the Hangover

In 1996 I am worn out and my face looks terrible. And so I agree to start the medications for AIDS, but I only take them for a few months due to the intense side-effects I experienced.

Within a few hours of taking the first pills I was extremely nauseas and had the shakes. My entire body was slightly vibrating. This shaking was constant and just one more thing that I could not escape. On this medication I vomited regularly and sometimes was sick out of the car door or through the car window. I experienced dry heaves that were so draining on my body that I quickly weakened and lost a lot of weight. I was not doing well on these toxic medications. Cal and I quickly realized that the respite that we sought was not within these drugs, but we felt I had no choice as was too weak, and so I continued. I now felt worse taking these drugs than I did when I was not taking them. After a few weeks on these medications I was a *space cadet*. I was physically numb and slow-witted. I realized later that the dosage being prescribed for HIV and AIDS was too strong. While on these drugs it felt as though I were peering out at the world through a bank of fog, and unsuccessfully measuring my surroundings. I was bumping into everything, even at work, and I was so incredibly nauseous. This is a nausea that when the wave of nausea arrives you can only stop and grasp the wall and wait for it to subside hoping not to vomit or pass out. It is truly a wave of madness. When the wave hits you are helpless as the body attempts to manage the toxicity of the drugs.

These drugs of AIDS are essentially an internal, weak chemotherapy that compounds over time. So instead of a few powerful blasts of radiation after which the body may then slowly heal. With the *Cocktail,* the combination of medications that are prescribed for HIV or AIDS, the body is filled with and radiated continually with a weaker form of chemotherapy and this never allows the body to rest or heal. And so the toxicity builds and the immune system weakens even more.

I remember a Thanksgiving when I was extremely ill. Cal and I were expected at my parent's house for dinner and though I felt horrible. I did not want to let my family down so we went. You see I am the middle child of our family, and with this there is a natural balance concerning the family dynamic. Growing up I mostly organized family get-togethers, Christmas', and more while living at home.

Let me say that it has been beautiful observing my brother and sister now being these qualities of love, family, organization, and communal understanding.

So Cal and I were returning home from my parent's house after a marvelous dinner and I got sick, really sick. We had experienced a lovely meal with my family. But afterwards as we were driving home I was feeling more miserable than usual because eating exacerbated my condition. The food would carry the medicines rapidly into my bloodstream and overwhelm my systems. After I ate the medication's side-effects intensified, including nausea.

That night on the way home from my parent's house we needed to stop to refill one of my prescriptions and I was at my breaking point. The medicine was compounding within me and each minute was more unbearable than the last. When we pulled into the pharmacy parking-lot I told Cal how terrible I felt and I opened my car door and threw up the entire Thanksgiving dinner onto the asphalt. This was a body-emptying purge that lasted for minutes. Cal was irate at this sight. Cal was through with seeing me suffer so he said "These drugs are not helping your quality of life my love. You are miserable and we can stop taking them if you want to. I understand completely and I love you. We will figure this out. I want you to be happy. We will do this together." Cal is a golden angel. I stopped taking medications (for the first time) that night.

Be

16

Suffering: The Late 1990's through 2004

Around 1998 I still experience rashes and strong allergies but I also start to have incredible, possibly stress-induced migraines that render me immobile. These migraines were torture. I would feel a slight pain in my cheekbone, become dizzy, and then slightly stumble as I reached for the wall. I realized then that I had about 15 minutes to get to a dark room and lie down before being paralyzed by pain. And if I did get to a dark room and lay down quick enough the pain would pass in only a few hours. But if I did not lie down soon enough the pain would last a solid day or more. Thank God that I only lived a few minutes from our home during those intense times because I could quickly drive home and find a darkened space.

I suffered with intense facial-bone migraines for approximately two years and then intermittently for another few years. There was never a medical diagnosis for these migraines. I attributed them to my inflamed and overwhelmed nerves that ran along my cheeks and my jaw bone. I do not really know. I was experiencing *TMJ: Temporomandibular Disorder* which caused swelling, clicking, and pain at the hinge of my jaw and so that could have easily caused the migraines.

I also realize that I was overloaded with energy from the past suffering and that I did also have that nervous breakdown. So having overwhelmed nerves in my skull seemed logical. Through the late 1990's I still manage to work, play, and perform in local bands but my energy is slowly waning.

Because of my growing illness people often asked, especially my band-mates, "Why are you so tired all of the time Richie? You are so young and you should have tons of energy. What's up?" They seemed to think that I was lazy or apathetic, but they were unaware of what I had been through so far and what was now happening below the surface of my life. Because I had not disclosed my disease to them I did not blame them. My friends did not know my history or my condition so I tried to act like nothing was wrong which was more stressful and required so much energy and continued to fracture my psyche.

I was on one hand all but destroyed, *fighting* AIDS and fighting to stay alive and sane and on the other I was a young intelligent musician in bands with a job. I pretended to be healthy and happy when if they only

knew my past and present they would have understood. I was still living a complex lie. But now I had disclosed that I was gay so the dual life-existence-stress was alleviated.

My friends thought that I was *normal* but I was losing energy. I was losing my battle. I needed rest even though I was only in my upper 20's. I needed some space to breathe in. I needed a respite from the storms of my past and the intensifying storm that I was in. I needed to heal. I simply needed energy.

Over the next few years I learn to live with my body and its limitations from illness. I am enjoying my day jobs and my musical projects and loving my life with Cal. But I am also now suffering incredible constant allergies and living on *Benadryl* which is incredibly disorienting. Taking *Benadryl* each day caused me to be perpetually slightly groggy, but I am still managing. I consistently have painful facial and scalp dermatitis and also 1 to 2" painful boils on my back but I can handle this too. I am not on any medications for AIDS or seeing a doctor. I am sleeping more and more, still fading and still barely *normal* until...

Love

17

AIDS; Beyond the Edge and Over the Ledge

My life turns from just barely *normal,* from that of a person living with *Advanced HIV Disease* to that of a victim of AIDS. In 2003 I was diagnosed with *full-blown* AIDS which means a person having less than 200 T-cells. That is all the doctor needed to know to state that I had AIDS. There we no other tests. Let me note that this cell count was measured after I experienced an extensive snowboarding injury in 2001 that put me in a soft-body cast and rendered me bed-ridden for months. And so again a low t-cell count should have been taken into consideration, but it wasn't.

Let us step back in a time a bit. In 2001 after my snowboarding injury and during the months of healing my body atrophies alarmingly and this is not the only time this occurs. I am weak, so weak that I cannot take physical steps without assistance. After the accident and within the body cast I cannot even stand on my own. The pain is incredible. Everything in my left shoulder area was crushed, torn, or stretched.

I am terribly weak. The left collarbone has been crushed beyond surgical repair with shattered bone-splinters lodged throughout my pectoral muscles. The bruise covering my torso was a sight to behold. I was half blue! Tendons and ligaments attached to the collar bone, shoulder, upper back, and triceps were either torn or hyper-extended. Every nerve was involved and how they complained. Let me state that when we move our foot the shoulder knows this. But throughout my incredible Calvin is everything to and for me. Being so weak I could not shower on my own, change my own clothes, dress my wounds, and let alone move without Cal's strength and assistance. It is months before I can walk a few house-lengths down the street. I am skin and bones and unknowingly now have full-blown AIDS.

This snowboarding injury compounded my already damaged immune system so I was now physically and spiritually broken. I eventually heal to 100% mobility with my shoulder and arm due to the belief that I would heal despite the level of injury I incurred. Actually, there was no limiting belief stating that my arm would not heal and so I healed. Is it not so interesting that a broken bone heals but that a tumor does not? Though my shoulder finally healed after about three years, this injury was the beginning of my decline into an indescribable darkness.

Be

18

Lesions, Dysplasia, and Fistulas

From the years 2003 up through 2005 I developed colon lesions and *Aggressive Dysplasia: A pre-cancerous abnormality of the cell* which multiplied and metastasized from my having no immune system, or energy to combat it. I require multiple operations to remove these lesions and growths, each operation and anesthetic further weakening my already damaged immune system. The storm intensifies.

The first removal of lesions was done by an insensitive doctor who burned with a laser the entire lining of my lower colon and rectum. I was raw. This was overwhelming pain. There was not just one localized painful area but my entire rectal lining and lower colon were burned away. They had also failed to inform me of the packing of gauze and cloth that was still inside me after the surgery. The discomfort and pain I felt is indescribable, especially as I unknowingly attempted to facilitate through the cloth and gauze packing. I did not

know that there was packing inside me so I pushed even harder, and this pain is beyond comprehension. You can imagine what using the bathroom would be like through burnt tissue – razors. I passed out more than once from that pain.

After this first removal of growths I then develop two *Anal Fistulas: An abnormal connection or passageway between two Epithelium lined organs or vessels that normally do not connect.* I require multiple surgeries.

What occurred is that a growth in my colon became infected. And my doctor suspected that it was a developing *Fistula* but was unable to externally treat it as at that point there was no external wound. Let me interject by sharing that this *Dr. S.* with whom I partnered throughout these rectal issues was and *is* amazing. He is a present and passionate man and I was honored to be treated by him.

Continuing, I had been experiencing a small *bubble* under the skin near my tailbone for some years. I lived with this *bubble* without much pain but then it expanded and sitting was uncomfortable. The *bubble under the skin* would also seem to internally fill with air and I would then need to manually push into that area and the *bubble* would then empty. At one point it became too painful to *empty* the *bubble* as I usually did so I stopped. *The bubble* then became hot and it felt like it was filled with more than air. The skin was red and appeared angry and resembled an infected blister. Now I could not sit without the aid of a pillow or cushion. I had gone to see *Dr. S.* and he stated that he could not do anything until the *Fistula* declared itself, or until it bursts. I could only wait anxiously for this bursting to happen and this did not take long. I was waiting for something to explode?

A few weeks later I began to experience consistent low-grade fevers so Cal and I knew that something was occurring. We assumed it was the infection of the *fistula* because the *bubble* was now always full of something, and very painful. The skin was angry, tight, and hot to the touch. We could now assume that this was a *Fistula* and that it would soon declare itself, or again soon burst.

Cal was out of town when the *Fistula* burst and I felt bad that he would feel bad that he was not at home being the loving angel that he is. I was lying in our bed in a pool of sweat in tremendous agony when it happened. The *bubble* was now incredibly painful. I could not touch that part of my skin to anything (including the mattress) so I was propped up uncomfortably onto my side. Lying there in bed it felt like acid was being placed drop by drop onto the *bubble*. I had a fever too high to share with Cal and I was basically passing in and out of consciousness from the excruciating pain. When "Bam!" it felt like a bomb went off. I realized that the fistula declared itself. OK, this was one of the most painful and uncomfortable (and messy)

moments I have endured, and as we learn I have had many moments.

I later found out that what had occurred is that the infection in my colon had created a toxic fluid that ate through the colon wall and eventually through the rectal muscles. The *bubble* had been formed by the final layers of skin being pushed up from below by the toxic liquid before the *fistula* declared itself or actually exploded through the skin of my inner-thigh. The infected fluid was consuming me in slow-motion. No wonder it hurt. The infected fluid then ate through the rectal wall, the muscles, and out through the skin leaving dead tissue along the way which resembled a wormhole in a fallen log.

These were unbelievably painful times. This was more pain weakening my immune system and sending me deeper into myself. This irony is that this suffering assisted me in transcending my limited ideas of suffering. Each new pain was part a continual slow detachment from the life I had known and into more of the oneness we are.

To clarify, after the *Fistula* declared itself the dead tissue then needed to be removed or cut out because the tissue was dead and would not heal. And if the tissue was not entirely removed it would then drain seeing that the opening was now *communicating* with the rectum.

In one of my surgeries they looped a nylon cord around the ring of the rectal muscle. I was then required to pull the nylon cord that was exiting out of my body through the *fistula*, or through the wormhole. This cord had been tied around the interior ring of the rectum and so as I pulled it slowly cut into and eventually through the rectal muscle. This action split my entire rectum and the wormhole (or the *Fistula*) in about three weeks, this allowing the hole to eventually close. What a shock when I pulled the final tug to then be holding the entirely exited nylon cord. These *Fistulas*, surgeries, and procedures that addressed them sent intense blows to my already poor, struggling, and energy-depleted immune system. I am fading.

I remember one moment when I was crying after being in so much pain from having to facilitate through open wounds. I could not avoid using the bathroom daily and *each* time was excruciating. I told Cal that I was glad that we did not own a gun and I meant it. I was miserable and in so much pain; pain that causes you to blackout from the overload; pain that it so powerful you cannot even cry, you just sit there disconnected wondering if you will make it back out of the darkness, and if you really want to.

During the surgeries a large amount of tissue was removed, about 4" long, 2" wide, and 1" deep. It took years for me to be able to sit normally.

After approximately six weeks being out on work-leave due to my surgeries I return to work. I am still employed as a *Civil CAD Operator* with sitting being the majority of my day which has now become unbearable due to the location of my surgeries. I try and work as long as I able but exacerbate my health by returning to work too soon. I do bring in a pillow to work to sit on but even this is not enough. Returning too soon back to work caused another *fistula* to develop that then required another surgery sending me bed-ridden again.

I lose my job from taking too many leaves of absence which exhausts my FMLA (Family Medical Leave).

Love

19

Another "Cocktail"

I was now barely alive. After losing three lovers to AIDS, the snowboarding accident, skin cancer (discussed later in the book), my *fistulas,* and whatever other illnesses I incurred up to that time there was little of me left. Cal was more than worried about me. He told me that when he looked into my eyes there was no light. I was dying. I was distant. I was drained and I did not care. I did not have the energy to care. The creative and vibrant man Cal had married was just not there. I had been replaced with some limp and drained *thing*. Concerning my health and survival at that point I numbly agreed to whatever Cal decided. I assumed that I was going to die (but not really completely sure) and I wanted Cal to be at peace with the entire situation.

Due to the increasing frequency of body ailments, the lack of light in my eyes, and the realization that I am now close to death Cal does the only thing he knows to do to save my life and he takes me to see another HIV/AIDS doctor. When I went to see my new infectious disease doctor, *Dr. B.*, I was near death. I was a sight to behold. I was skinny and grey and I could sense the alarm when he met and spoke with me, but I also sensed his hope. I had receded so deep into myself that most of me was not *there* in my body. I seemed to be floating and observing. I was detached but I did feel his light.

So In 2004 I start the *cocktail* for AIDS a second time and do experience a slight elevation of energy. Let me say that at this time the medications were exactly what I needed since they are what I took. I believed that the medications would help me and so they did, up unto a point.

I do experience a short reprieve in that there is a noticeable increase in my energy. But the medications prescribed were too toxic. And I again experience intense physical side-effects similar to the first time that I took them, but some also unique. To begin with I experience a slight and constant physical tremor. And I am also perpetually nauseas and vomiting daily. I also experience a mysterious psychological affect that was like a form of *Claustrophobia: A fear of being in confined spaces*. And that sucked. I could not be in a closed room or car without having a panic attack. As we drove the car the windows needed to be cracked open or I felt that I would crack.

I also experienced the most dreadful and dark sleeping (and awake) nightmares or thoughts that would loop in my mind without resolution, and which seemed beyond my control. In disbelief after some research into my prescriptions I realized that experiencing *nightmares* was one of the many accepted side-effects of one of the medications that I was taking. Incredulously I wondered "What is a nightmare? Isn't a nightmare unique for each individual? How is a drug creating nightmares within my mind? I cannot believe an accepted side-effect is one that causes nightmares. What the hell am I taking?" I was overwhelmed. I was dying. I was bed-ridden and I was over it.

In summary, in 2004 I started the *cocktail* prescribed for AIDS and then stopped permanently on January 26, 2006.

I am not telling anyone to stop taking their prescriptions. I am here sharing my experience with AIDS medications and expressing that a person needs to be aware of all that they are in-taking, including their medications. I am not a doctor. Please consult your support team and your heart for your own decisions concerning your medical care.

Research AIDS to find your own understanding.

Use this book as a reference and inspiration.

Let your heart guide you through these pages.

Be

20

Skin Cancer and Stopping Medications

The suffering for me continues. In 2004 I had a large 1.5 cm diameter and aggressive skin cancer removed from my forehead. This required four separate plastic surgeries that same day to remove all of the cancerous tissue and to also minimize the scarring. I still have a noticeable 2" scar. I felt terrible after each surgery seeing that there were more bandages applied after each procedure and Cal was worried enough as it was without seeing more bandages.

When I walked out to see him in the waiting-room he would see the accumulating bandages and worry even more. After the first surgery there was only a small bandage about 3" square covering the open wound. But after the fourth surgery and upon my fourth return to the waiting-room my entire head was covered with bandages and Cal had no idea what was under those bandages.

During a surgery they would take a new tissue sample and send it to the lab. We would wait for the results in the waiting-room. "Is there more cancer to remove? Yes", and so back into surgery I went. I required a total of four surgeries that long and arduous day. I required multiple internal and external stitches.

I remember one surreal moment when an assistant was splitting the skin of my scalp to stretch the new skin over the open wound. My left eyebrow and ear pulled an inch higher as a result. The doctor placed his knee into my chest for leverage so he could grab and tighten my scalp for the staples. And because he anchored so deep with his weight into my body my chest was sore for days. I was even bruised on my shoulders from the assistants holding me into the chair as the doctor pulled at my skin. It was surreal. I needed a valium before each surgery.

I knew that one day I would stop taking the medications prescribed for AIDS. I was getting stronger, becoming clear, and feeling peaceful. I had thought about stopping the drugs many times during 2005 but it was not a knowing. I did not *know* that I was ready to stop. I did not feel good on these drugs physically or consciously and I was slowly feeling better overall but it was not the *time* to quit. I can put it that I was somehow aware of an approaching energetic balance in my life, though not really sure how. Then one day in an instant I knew that I was done with my medications for AIDS.

I clearly recall flipping open the lid on the pill organizer on the morning of January 26, 2006, and when shaking the pills out into my hand I froze. I was observing the pills in my hand from a space of more than AIDS. This was the day. I knew that I did not on any level *need* these medications anymore. I returned the pills to the container and waited for Cal to come so that we could talk.

There was no argument or discussion. Cal could sense the knowing from me and we agreed that I was done with the maintenance medications for AIDS. I have taken other medications after this fact briefly, as with the double-pneumonia, but this was basically for my body and for those in my life's benefit because I was free throughout the experience.

I stopped taking maintenance drugs as I was now maintained by Love.

Love

21

What is Really Happening?

Back In 2004 I knew that my life needed to change. I realized that I needed to change. I needed to know what was really going on and what it was that was causing my disease. I had so many questions. "What is AIDS? Where did AIDS come from? Do people live long after being *full-blown*? Are there long-time survivors of *full-blown* AIDS? What is HIV? What is its role with AIDS?"

Again, I am not here to tell you what AIDS is or how to *cure* AIDS. Do the research you need into HIV and AIDS for your own harmony. I am here to show that we are more than AIDS or a dis-ease and as this awareness we are cured.

In 2004 after my skin cancer removal I was inspired to become a vegetarian. Actually I became a *Vegan: no animal products consumed.* I began meditating and something within me began to change, or maybe expand is a better way to put it. There seemed to be a small space for me to breathe in when I meditated that was not there

(or of which I was not aware of) when I was not meditating and it was incredible. It felt that after all of this time I had discovered a magic place in which I could sit and be *away* from the world and most importantly, my suffering.

At this time in meditation when I observed my mind it was pure chaos. Imagine non-stop layers of trains of thoughts overlapping and zooming in and out in all directions and you begin to experience my mind. I was overloaded with thinking and not experiencing any sanctuary.

While meditating there was the smallest ray of light making its way into the *cavern of my misery* and this light was important in that it was a symbol of hope. This was an *interior* light that I had not known before, because it was dark where I was, unimaginably dark. I instinctually knew that the more space I created within through meditation, the more light I would know in my life. I needed illumination. My life needed illumination. I needed to see my way out of the abyss, and meditation became my lantern.

Let me share that there is not an instant change in our lives through meditation. It is a gradual expansion of our consciousness; a spiraling. Trying to anticipate what will be experienced in meditation is wasting energy. We only need to sit and observe and Love will do the rest.

When we open and surrender to the interior space, we become what is and of that space.

Be

22

We Are Not Allergic, We Are Toxic

I was now a Vegan, meditating daily, and slowly centering my life but I still incur minor illness after minor illness. I also have a non-stop allergy (or so my limited thinking assumed) that is taking me through two boxes of *Kleenex* a day for almost two years. This constant sneezing in itself is exhausting and most maddening. I sneeze hundreds of times a day, every day. My nose continually runs and bleeds from the blowing.

I have learned that what we label as an allergy is one of the many ways in which the body detoxifies. The body utilizes mucus to contain the toxins in our body. The mucus membranes then transport the toxins out of our body via the mucus. I realized that sneezing and having a runny nose are actually gifts because with each sneeze the body was expelling toxins.

We are not benefited to halt this natural detoxification and cleansing process of the body. Because when we take

pills or do anything that stops our noses from running or stifles our sneezing we are stopping the mucus flow that is carrying the toxins and waste out of our body and we only compound our toxicity. Through our medications we are literally saying *"be quiet"* to the body and remaining toxic.

Listen to the body. The body is telling us through our allergies that we are toxic. So I stopped taking my allergy medicines mid 2004, sneezed and had colds for approximately two more years and then all of my *symptoms* subsided. I addressed the source of my allergies and not just the symptoms. I addressed the toxicity. Today I do not experience these *allergies* because today I am not toxic.

I also realized that I would become congested after eating certain (toxic) foods, or after a bought of depression (toxic), and even after becoming angry (toxic). I also stopped the medications for AIDS and so stopped that intake of toxicity as well. I also realized that some extended family members became *sick* at the same times, especially through the holidays. I understood that when we habitually eat too much or add to much toxicity to the body we then get flues, colds, and more.

How many people do we know that become ill after or during the holidays, many. Do we think that non-thinking organisms such as bacteria annually gather and attack us? No, this is illogical. These organisms do not have this

capacity of intelligence. What occurs is that we eat heavy and processed (toxic) foods and become over-loaded. Our body *puts* us to bed with a cold, flu. We then experience a mucus overload until the mucus completes its job of detoxification, or is prematurely halted by a medication and we heal. But we need to stop the toxicity so the body can catch up.

This is why we have no appetite when we do not feel well because the body has essentially *turned* our hunger off so it has enough energy to do what it needs to do.

Love

23

Insight into Dis-ease and Cancer

Please note that this is purely my hypothetical understanding concerning energy, cancer development, and tumors. I am not advising anyone to ignore a tumor or any health situation. I am adding more dimension to the cancer scenario. I am adding another perspective that one may take or leave concerning their health and life journey.

Cancer is not attacking us. The body has collected too much heavy metal and toxins and it is now storing them in the bone, muscle, skin, or whatever is convenient for the body. The body does not want to transport these toxins through the blood-stream so it will utilize the closest organ or tissue to collect and contain these toxins until it has enough energy to assimilate and purge. The problem is that we are so depleted of energy that our body is too overwhelmed to try and *clean* and *heal* us so the body may ignore a tumor for some time. And this is not right or wrong, this is how the body works. It uses energy, and if it does not have enough energy it slows and becomes

overloaded. And also what happens is that when we discover a location where the body is temporarily storing its toxins we do not listen to the body. We do not realize that the body is conveying to us through the tumor that we are toxic. No, we label it as a tumor and then proceed to cut it out. We need to realize that the little energy we are providing the body with is not enough to run all of its processes and so a tumor may exist in the body for some time and this is fine. When we lessen the toxicity in our lives we provide the needed energy to the body so it may dispel the toxicity and in the process heal us.

The body's relationship with cancer is akin to us placing items in a box for a future project and then storing it in a closet. We may never get to the stored project seeing that we are too busy. And this is analogous to how the body may never get to the tumor because it is too busy.

There is no mystery to this process. We need to increase our energy and the body will then have the fuel it needs to address the tumor and our toxicity and we will achieve optimal health.

Be

24

Body Language and Double Pneumonia

Since being a Vegan and a Raw *Foodist,* and after the toxicity in my body leveled I do not experience colds or flu-like symptoms like before. Cal is also a vegetarian eating meat occasionally and he has not had colds or flues as frequently either. I may feel heavier physically and sometimes slightly congested after a vegetarian meal, especially cheese, and this is the body's language sharing that what I had eaten requires cleaning. I am listening to my body.

We are what we consume and in multi-dimensional ways.

Fevers are also part of the language of our body. During a fever the body is raising its temperature to essentially *cook* and kill off the bugs and toxins it is overwhelmed by. I have listened to many fevers. We need to listen to the body because it never ceases speaking to us and loving us. I cannot stress enough to become aware of the body and how this awareness will open up new doors of wonder.

Our perception and awareness determine the relationship we have with our body.

So concerning my healing, around late 2004 I seem to be experiencing something *wrong* with my body like clockwork, about every three weeks. But even in this flow of non-stop physical illnesses something is happening in the background of my consciousness. I know that on some level I am healing and that I am *more* than AIDS. I am sneezing less. I have more energy. I am thinking less about death. Actually, I am just thinking less. A part of me is inaudibly and in some mysterious way comforting me and I somehow feel more of me. And this more of me is giving me the understanding that all of this suffering needs to occur for me to heal and to be whole.

My inner voice says "Have patience so as not to be a patient."

Jumping ahead, I was hospitalized in September of 2007 with the *dreaded* double-pneumonia but I was fearless. I knew my wholeness. I was aware. I had been experiencing fevers of up to 104 degrees for more than a week from heavy, heavy detoxifying and that was that. I had also alarmingly lost about 15 pounds in 5 days from my already skinny body and was a mere skeleton but I did not care. I was also experiencing intense physical burning

in my upper lungs that I had not experienced before and this was OK too. When I inhaled a deep breath I would experience dry heaves through razor-like pain as I fought for air but through it all of these symptoms of suffering I was observing unattached. And I knew that what was happening was happening out of love and for my body's benefit. I was not worried. I was at peace. I was and am now *more* than the body. I was letting my body freely clean and detoxify without hindering it with my limited beliefs. I knew that my previous beliefs had been impeding the detoxifying process and so now I would heal.

With this double pneumonia my fevers were very high and constant. My body would convulse and shake from this high temperature. Cal was in shock. He was barely able to watch me endure as I *cooked,* but *I* was unaffected. I was observing from a place of knowing more than suffering. I knew oneness and so did not complain. I was smiling through my rattling teeth. I did not fret, cry, or have any anger because one can only be angry at *things,* and *things* I am *more* than.

And though my doctor talked with me about my *Living Will,* my impending death, and the fact that I would most-likely not make it out of the hospital this time, I was in and out in five days and healthy in three months. I believed, no, I *knew* that I was free, and *that* was the key to me healing. I knew that our body is ephemeral and that it will change and eventually energetically transmute and this is beautiful. We are the caterpillar *and* the butterfly. I knew that I was more than the body, and seeing I knew, I was free.

Within wholeness there is nothing to attach to. Wholeness IS.

I was observing my body use the lungs to clear and transport toxins through the mucus and I understood why. I also knew that this was only a thought and that I did not care about the details of what was happening. I did not need to define what was happening, just *be*. I was at peace throughout.

I now knew more than suffering and the purifying and harmonizing of my *AIDS Consciousness* was integral in this realization. I did not add anything to the situation of pneumonia so my body could then perform in the way it needed without my thinking getting in the way. My thinking, which is energy, was not denying the body of its needed energy to heal. I flowed through the decisions for me to take medicines and then through the decision for me to enter the hospital. I observed being in a hermetically-sealed room for fear that I may have tuberculosis. I observed as my body used every ounce of energy to expectorate the stubborn phlegm. I observed the blood being taken every few hours as they monitored my body and the endless procession of medications behind administered. I observed it all.

Let us realize that our body is intelligent and self-healing. We do not have to think about our heartbeat right, or our digestion, or any of the other millions of processes that our glorious body takes care of. Put simply, my body was purging through my lungs, end of story. I was present. I was not feeding any illusory thoughts about AIDS or creating any new limiting beliefs concerning pneumonia. My body with the assistance of the medications healed.

Today I do not take any medications. I have energy. I am here, creative, vital, aware, and available. I am not adverse to medicine and do *not* tell anyone what they should or should not do. I may take medications again in the future for the body, I do not know. I will know then.

I am now a mirror so that all may see themselves before, during, and after AIDS (or *AIDS Consciousness)*, suffering, death, fear, and depression.

I am here now, and I can only thank AIDS and *AIDS consciousness* for showing me myself through suffering. I know not what tomorrow brings, for the gift is here and now in the present.

Today is all I know. Today is all that is and it is what I offer you now. I know that the body is designed to heal itself and that it is fully automated and I am now *out of the way*. My body may now *be* because I am free.

Part 3

The Steps Taken

Now that we have insight into my journey in, out, and beyond *AIDS Consciousness* let us walk together into the freedom, peace, and the realization that we are *m*ore than what we have accepted ourselves to be.

The remainder of this book describes the beginning steps that I took to becoming aware. What I share is not a medical cure because each person needs to follow their own inner-voice and take their exterior team into consideration concerning their suffering. What is within these pages is the silent love of which we are all a part, the part beyond words and paper illuminating a unique ray of light through me.

I humbly ask you to read each of the following sections slowly and openly. The words may seem simple and the explanations amateur or elementary and this is fine.

It is the simple things that are easy to understand and which have the greatest affect. Know that each letter, word, and the spaces in-between are infused with my heart. I am here offering more. In this book I hope you find what you seek through an open heart and quiet mind.

I traveled through agony, and now through my understanding others may not have to.

We may know the waves of the ocean from the perspective of drowning or from the tranquil shore.

They are the same waves.

Love

25

Toxicity and Tasting Awareness

As I have shared, it is a toxic lifestyle that germinates the seed of our suffering within our consciousness. Our limited lifestyle and level of SELF-misunderstanding is what is creating our dis-ease. And so it is the energetic inner *architecture* of our consciousness that shapes our reality. It is our toxic thoughts and beliefs that are the building-blocks of our suffering. Let me share that we are energy *and* that we are more than energy. We are light and we are more than light. Within our scientific understanding we now know that at our most fundamental core we are a part of a quantum vibrating field of energy potentials that we know is intelligent and self-serving, of which today we have myriad names, of the many I use God, love, and oneness and we are that.

Love: That which embraces and of which we are integral.

According to the information accepted by most institutions of wisdom such as Physics, Quantum

Mechanics, Mathematics, Religion, Modern and Ancient Spiritualities, and more, all of life is a form of consciousness. Life is an intelligent love that communicates through vibration, or through *spiritual* means.

We know that though we appear solid our body is actually approximately 97% empty intelligent awareness. We are approximately 98% space. Really sit with this information. You are not the body you are the space in which it is formed.

We are space, truly. And what we can now observe we are more than, and can we not observe any*thing*? We can observe all the parts of our body from a mysterious vantage point, yes? And so we are more. We can lose a hand, an arm, a leg, our eyes, our liver, our appendix, our heart, and more and we still are aware. We may even be deep in a dream not aware of the body and still we are aware. So we are then the one observer that is observing the movie of our life. We are more than any*thing*. We are the intelligent awareness of existence.

When we realize that we are more than the body we are then not limited by the body or any dis-ease. And with this realization we transcend the limitations we have concerning the body, including *AIDS Consciousness* and we are free.

Be

26

Realizing the Present Moment through our Body

As you awaken, the moment before you open your eyes pause and reflect upon what is being experienced. This is not the sameness that the mind protests and suggests it is, oh no. This is newness, and it is all here for you now. This morning is unique as are all mornings. We just don't realize the newness because we are looking through our ego, and not as pure awareness.

Thank Love, God, Goddess, the Universe, or whatever you thank for your life experience that you are again back in the dream of being an individual. You have arrived back in life at the exact same spot in which you *fell* asleep. Even *you* are new this morning, this moment, this now. Nothing is the same. The sheets are in a new wrinkle. The light is adorned in new shafts of dusty asymmetry. Even your cells are newly arranged. Through closed eyes when we feel deeply we can sense that we are being reborn when we pause just before we open our eyes.

We are born with each eye-opening and with each breath. Touching this knowing within before we open our eyes helps us to not step back into our routine or back into our habits. Then we experience the true moment.

Does this sound simple and silly? Well it is, and is this not great?

When a child arises the morning is fresh, vibrant, and pregnant with endless possibilities. What has changed? Why do we not experience this now? It is because deep in our personal stories, and not aware. Do you think it is advantageous to examine into this? I do.

Are you now the same awareness that observed throughout your childhood? Yes you are. Are you the same observer that watched you learning in school, getting your first job, meeting your first love, and more? Yes, you are this same awareness. You have always been here. The body may have changed and the world may have changed but the same observer has observed throughout. You *are*. We *are*. The body has morphed and changed but *you* are not the body. You are the same unwavering awareness that has always observed your life. So what has today changed to create your suffering? Your perception of life has changed. Your mind has changed. Your mind has filled with evolving knowledge, and instead of remaining the observer you forgot and you developed your ego and then the game of separation began. Your ego

then anchored itself into nature seeking its understanding when we now realize that eternal peace is not found in the shifting energies of creation. Eternal peace is beyond *things*. Eternal peace is being the observer, being aware.

Knowledge and facts have been stored as best as they could in our consciousness as we learned and re-remembered who we *are,* and now we are awakening and addressing our consciousness. Know that each time you close and open your eyes that everything is new, it truly is. And you can get in touch with this knowing through your body. Then the present moment is like the juice from the pulp of *now* running down your smiling face through the gratitude gleaned through knowing our body.

God bless our body.

As you open your eyes become aware of the body, but do this slowly. Understand the true meaning of gratitude. We are not obligatorily sending gratitude *out* to some unknown and mysterious *thing* in the *Kosmos*. No, we are so deeply rooted in our direct experience and the knowing that this body can carry and act out our every wish that we can barely contain this joy. We are grateful for having body-ability. Simply without the body we could not be here on Earth. We could not play the game of being individuals. We could not experience the light and sound vibration through our senses that the body provides and relays for us.

Without this divine vehicle we could not smell the dreamy fragrances of nature, the mustiness of another or the emptiness of the wind. Without smell we could not experience the multidimensionality of the food that we eat, the signature of approaching rains, or even a version of time travel through scent and memory association.

Or what if we had no eyes? Without eyes we could not have explosions of indescribable colors fill us till we near combustion. Without these magnificent eyes we could not see the indescribable pastel-pallet of a sunrise, the burning hues of a sunset, or the sparkling eyes of love in the eyes of another human being who loves us just because. We could not see the undulating waves on the water, in the trees, on the sand, or through the clouds. We could not see the ever-shifting and ever-giving kaleidoscope of light, and if we had no ears?

Without ears we could not hear the words "I love you." We could not hear the melodic songs of singers, chanters, or frogs. We could not hear the rumbling thunder or the sound of rain dancing onto flat stones or metal roof. We could not experience the music of prayers, the harmony of our conversations, or the sounds of musical instruments. We could also not hear the sobbing of our suffering or the laughter of our Joy. We could not hear.

What?

Are we starting to understand gratitude? There is no guilt involved here we are only observing, detach...

Without hands we could not caress or comfort. We could not raise our children or each other when in need. We could not nestle with puppies, plant seeds in the soil, or play musical instruments. We could not express ourselves through artistic mediums such as painting or sculpture. We could not even feed ourselves.

What if we had no hands?

Just imagine as you look at your delicate and amazingly evolutionarily-designed hands what they mean to your life. Examine the bones the muscles and tissue connections. See how the hand bends, grasps, and spreads, the design is beyond description. Realize that if we only lost one finger our life is altered significantly.

This is not drama it is the way to realize oneness through gratitude of the present moment through the body. This exercise of presence can go on forever. Practice this gratitude exercise and you will feel the vibration of gratitude vibrate in every cell of your body. You will experience and know gratitude intimately. You will realize gratitude.

How much do we take for granted through lives of sameness and disconnection? What about the interior of our body? Without our organs we would cease to function. Imagine how loved we are that we can eat whatever we want and our body will digest, assimilate it for us. The body even *tells* us when we have become toxic so that we may consciously evolve - astounding!

Our body does all of the work for us and we only need to neutrally observe. Our body even heals itself so that we may continue observing the glorious river of love. We do not need to do anything. We do not have to worry if certain enzymes are being carried through the bloodstream or if the heart is beating or if our bone marrow is creating enough red or white blood cells or if there are the correct hormones being released or what to do with the billions of dying and birthing cells. We are so loved that we don't even have to breathe because the body is breathing for us. We can just sit in observation without thinking about the body or its incalculable operations and just *be*.

Do you think we should love this body? Oh yes we should.

God is the body. Love is the body. Cherish the body.

So move the body and help the body by listening to it. And when the body requests something assist the body though cessation, stillness, or mobility. Be sensitive. Stretch the body. Strengthen the body. Utilize the body. The body understands and enjoys these activities. When

feed the body life it thrives. Run, dance, skip, climb, lift, wrestle, jump, play, jog, make love and be in the body. This body can be your wildest dream so fly.

All is provided is a powerful pointer to realizing our wholeness. All that we need to do is to be grateful for the moment and observe this bountiful and humbling gift of life that we are forever receiving though the glorious body.

Oneness is beyond our current understanding so we don't need to understand it, just be it. *Love* loves us so much, and actually *we* love ourselves so much that anything we could ever need is provided, anything at all at any level and we only need to be aware.

Love

27

Tasting the Present of Presence

As we listen attentively with our eyes open to the sounds of where we are and then close our eyes and reopen them we realize that this is a new experience. So through this exercise we ground into the present moment. We realize *now*. We ground in and beyond the body through the body and this is amazing.

The record of life is spiraling for infinity. It does not stop and then restart. This is only what the mind does and not the river of *now*. The mind recreates sections of the past or sections of a projected future and then our lives are analogous to a skipping record. We live the same experience over and over and we stagnate. As the river of love flows onward we are living in illusion. We are living in a fantasy timeline.

The body is an eternal door to the present.

The body is here now. We can imagine (or fantasize) that we have a cut on our arm but our body illumines this

fallacy to us. We can envision the wound and convince ourselves that we have a cut, but when we observe the arm there is no cut. In this way the body is the *way* back to the present.

As we listen and ground into life through the body we become more aware and hear new animal songs and calls. There are new mechanistic whirs, bangs, beeps, grinds, creaks, and more. There are different frequencies of tones and hums abounding, and even in silence there are waves of variance. Within the emptiness are gossamer waves of knowing that are like silk wings caressing our soul.

Nothing happening is the same. It is only our mind that is replaying programs of the past and the projected future which is creating an illusion of sameness. This then stales, dulls, and distorts our life experience. It is akin to a person spending their life sitting and staring at a small scene being played out on a table in a room when outside of that room there is a never-ending play of newness with a scope unknown. Let us through awareness *be* outside of that room.

Now that we have connected deeply with the body through this exercise of gratitude rise from where you sleep and feel the awakening of your muscles, joints, organs, bones, and more as you stand.

Connect with the body in a silent knowing of thanks and begin your day. Feel the floor and the shifting of your feet as you walk. Notice the angles of the walls and doorways shifting and bending as you move, or as *they* move by you. Observe the angles of sunlight as they spread and dance in through the windows. Listen to the shapes of the rooms and how the spaces sound and feel differently as you walk.

As you prepare for work or play utilize the body to stay aware. Remain aware. Be aware of the depth of your breath and the clearness of your mind as you wash your sacred body. Love your body as you clean, and not because you are supposed to clean your body but because you love your body. You are simply grateful.

Every brush of the cloth, swipe of the soap, and splash of water is the language our body recognizes. Be present and observe as you shower or bathe.

Languages are not only in the forms of sounds or words, they are also known through feelings.

Love your body because it has carried you up until this point in your life healing your fevers, hangovers, broken bones, heartaches, and more and will continue to do so just because it loves you, because *you* love you.

Look at yourself deeply in the mirror as you brush your teeth or shave, really look, for you are amazing. See yourself. See US. See the oneness. Stay aware.

Stay grounded as you prepare your morning meal. Smell the aromatic food and feel the shiny, hard utensil in your hand. Observe your mind as the thoughts and programs begin loading in the background as your mind staggers awake. And through observing these programs and not being a part of these programs the programs will cease to run. Being present you are habit-free and deprogrammed as well. Habits are rooted in the past, and through the body we realize the present and so less habits.

You are now free of these programs because you have observed them. At this point in your life it now only takes discipline and continued practice to dismantle your habits. This can be achieved through body awareness, meditation, contemplation, Yoga, prayer, and more.

Create silence daily to connect with the witness of your experience and ground into the moment through your body. By way of inner observation habitual and limiting programs of the mind will quell and you will taste oneness.

Be

28

Gratitude: A Gateway to Grace

Let us deepen into our gratitude through utilizing the practice of body awareness to realize the present moment. Let us remain in a state of awareness throughout our day by being grateful for the body. We are not *thinking* about how to remain aware as we run errands, work, play, etc. We are remaining aware in the now through awareness of our body through the senses.

The more present we are the richer our life experience.

Try driving your car in presence, or we may say try driving and being aware of driving while *being*. Today there are many terms for living in the moment that point to our oneness and *being* is one of them. Start the car and feel the vibrations. Feel your hand, (thank God for hands, right?) on the wheel, feel the temperature of the plastic, and the shape of the curving steering-wheel. Stay in *touch* with the moment through tactile sensations. Let's not listen to the radio today, OK? Now feel the way that your body sinks into the seat the longer that you sit in it. Now start your drive and stay aware.

Push down the gas pedal and feel the acceleration and the shifting weight of the car. Notice now how everything blends into one moving panoramic scene as you observe the whole view, and not only just the pieces. Try and look out through all of your eyes and not just out through the center. We tend to stare and live our lives directly out in front of us tense and concentrated and this has the effect of limiting what our eyes see and what our consciousness is aware of.

This is similar to focusing only on one part of a movie screen to observe an actor and the rest of the scene is not observed. We know the movie through the actor but not as it's entirely. We do have the ability to observe through our eyes wholly and this only requires practice. We may then see what is to the left of us, to the right of us, and at the center simultaneously. This is the way that our eyes are designed. Our eyes are spherical. But through our limiting habits we begin to see and experience our life through a type of tunnel-vision. We become linear. We are so focused on the future and the past that we are riding in a constricted tube of life experience.

We can use this as an example. As we are driving we observe that the faster the rate at which we travel the narrower our view then becomes. This is another simple

analogy for our life experience. We are unable to focus our eyes peripherally so we only concentrate on a small piece of the scene directly ahead of us. If we have traveled fast enough, say while skiing or in extreme action we have experienced our view reduced to a small tunnel just ahead of us as appearing as a small movie screen. To our sides is just a blur. This tunnel-vision is analogous to our limited awareness. When we are unaware or when we are not present we are moving quickly towards our fantasy away from the present moment. Our awareness is limited. We are then experiencing a blurring life. We are in a tunnel. We are not aware of the horizontal horizon or verticality of our life. We are precariously balancing on a thin line of linearity and we suffer. We are so intently focused on a possible distant future that our view becomes only of that possible future.

The power and clarity of awareness which we experience through being grounded through the body is that awareness *sees* through the total eye of life. Similar in that awareness sees or knows all of life at once. We are then aware of the horizontal and vertical aspects of our life experience simultaneously. We are aware of the sphere of our existence. We are aware of oneness. There is no tunnel even when we are at fast speeds because we are not limited by beliefs. We do not experience the *blur* that is created from attaching to illusion. We may see the blur, but we do not attach ourselves into the blur so we are then at peace no matter what the situation.

As we are driving in presence there are no individual pieces now that we have realized the puzzle of our life. All is one flow of love through our senses. So listen now to the engine symphony and the aria of the road surface as you drive. Hear the syncopated percussion of tires as you travel over the variances and seams in the road. Hear your breath and feel your heart. Realizing this sensitive ability is possible the more deeply you observe. There are countless sounds drowned out by the incessant chatter of the mind that will surface and resound when we are present.

Let people be exactly who they are in the other cars as you experience the drive to work. Can you *feel* how thick and alive the drive is becoming? Can you feel the emptiness of not worrying about others or of anything but the drive?

Let the traffic be, as it does not concern you now. You are free. Expect nothing and you are never let down or upset. Support yourself and no one can drop you or let you down or push or upset you. People drive and cars zoom and that is that. Some drivers are late and some are early and just stay present. When someone cuts you off in traffic then they cut you off and now back to driving; back to the present. Don't become attached to them through anger because attachment does exactly what it states. It attaches you to some*thing* as the river of now continues flowing onward, and then you suffer as life pulls at you to continue flowing. Don't blame another to only then become enmeshed in their drama.

No collecting pieces just observe the flow.

Stay in the moment through acceptance and gratitude for all that occurs, not just what you *think* should occur. Anyone can have a bad day and then be irritable on the way to work we have all been the ego behind the wheel. Let them go on in their way as you observe unbiased. Observation is not attachment. Observation is eternal freedom. Observe the day. Observe the people at your work. Observe the swaying trees and the blue sky and be free. Let it all go. Let it all happen. Be grateful.

Again, when we are observing we are neutral. We are not dull or uninspired. And it is through our neutrality that we are unbridled in our inspiration. We then dance in our unfiltered pure awareness. We are passionate for the moment. We are inspired by *now*. We do not react through our egos but fully respond to the present. We are full of the potentials needed for any situation through our being present. And just as the body does all that is required for our health so too does oneness provide through our being aware.

Love

29

Simplifying and Centering our Lives

In order for us to know ourselves beyond our ego, or beyond our world created identity we need to see through the inner veils created from identifying through another's limitation. These veils of limited understanding include what we have learned through our well-meaning family members, from our friends, through the media, in the accepted beliefs of our time, and through the collective lineage of which we are a part.

We need to observe and understand these higher *levels* of harmony we are not currently aware of within ourselves so to then connect with our oneness. We need to create an environment that is conducive for this journey inward and we need to do this now to holistically heal. We need to connect with more than our ego to know the one that observes our ego.

To begin with we need to simplify our sensory intake so the flood of toxicity to our body lessens and we can

energetically balance. We can then utilize this energy now available to heal us.

Realize that all that we experience *is* energy and that this energy is continually processed and integrated as it enters and exits our body by and through our senses. Realize also that it requires energy to process and harmonize the energy flowing through our senses. And so the more distortive the energy that we are exposed to the more energy the body requires to harmonize these distortive waves of energy.

When we think of the energy that we are exposed to daily it is incredible that we can even maintain a sense of normalcy on this dynamic planet. As I am sitting here typing I know that the full spectrum of sound and light waves are passing through me on all levels. Though I am not consciously aware of the radio and light energy vibration bands passing through me, my body surely is. My body is eternally assimilating and harmonizing for my well being and this requires energy to do so.

In one day through our senses we may see the turquoise jewel of sky or the bloodiest of battles. We may hear the laughing of children, beautiful music, or the echoing of geese on the wind above. With the sense of touch we may feel the pain from an injury or the pain from a careless remark. We may hear ear-deafening jack hammers, construction sounds, car horns, or sirens, you name it and we are exposed to it and this is not healthy. These sights, sounds, and feelings affect our energy in powerful ways. And when we are not energetically balanced we suffer.

We can see that for a person with a properly functioning immune system it is enough just to make it through the day and back home energetically balanced. But for someone with a severely damaged immune system this sensory input requires energy to assimilate and this energy we do not have to spare.

With AIDS and all dis-ease we need to become hyper-sensitive as to what we are consuming with our eyes, ears, mouth, nose, and smell. Let us utilize our wisdom and only partake in harmonized energies such as loving, caring, happiness, peacefulness, nature, serving others (which helps us be in a space of observance), and uplifting music and words. Harmonized activities do not require energy to balance them because they are harmonized. Let us know harmony and create quiet in our lives so that what little energy we have available will be the fuel our body needs for healing. Let us construct our physical sanctuary to then know our inner-sanctuary.

Silence quenches every thirst and fulfills all desires.

Let us create a space to expand into the observer.

Love

30

Creating Our Sacred Space

Creating a sacred space is a personal and organic on-going process. All we need to do is find a place and just sit and the space will design itself. Find a quiet part of your home that will, if living with others or not be without interruption for the time set aside for your meditation. I will speak more on meditation in a few moments, hopefully demystifying and simplifying it for you. Let us now continue discussing a sacred space.

I found myself naturally meditating in our glassed-in three-season room during the warmer parts of the year and on the couch in the living-room during the winter. You may choose the best space for your heart. Consistency is the key concerning meditation so in the beginning the length of the sit is not important. You want to start out in small increments so as not to become too overwhelmed or disillusioned. Ten minute meditations are a good start. It is important that you meditate each day so that the root of your determination will be sown.

Then Love will pollinate your heart. Because when we open our experience mysteries pollinate our soul.

In our sacred space we may choose to decorate or adorn with inspiring and uplifting things to aid in our centering and conscious expansion. We may be inspired to place statues within our sacred space. We may place idols such as archetypes, saints (those who have lived before and whom we consider to be living now), deities, gods, and more representing the purity and love that we seek to realize, these things being mirrors into ourselves.

We may place photos of those living that we love and aspire to be. We may place images of those in whom we resonate or have physically met and also aspire to be. We may then create a small alter to hold these objects. We may also hang peaceful tapestries and paintings on the walls to help with the mood. We may drape tapestries across the top or sides of our alter also. We may light incense or sound bells before we meditate to cleanse the space, center our mind, and to open our heart. We will each create sacred spaces that reflect our uniqueness.

Let us be free with the creation of our sanctuary. This sanctuary represents who we are at *higher* levels of our awareness and so follow your heart and inspiration and let the sanctuary organically develop over time.

I did not intend to build the alter. I purchased a beautifully hand-painted concrete *Buddha,* the *Buddha* being one with whose suffering I strongly resonate and I placed this statue on top of my entertainment center in our living-room at eye-level. Over time I adorned the Buddha with mala prayer beads, rosaries, rings, necklaces, and bracelets that I had acquired which were spiritually significant to me.

I placed stones borrowed from peaceful rivers and tranquil locations and also arranged crystals such as Tibetan Quartz, amethyst, and citrine around and on Buddha. I also purchased a small golden bowl at *The 10,000 Buddha's Buddhist Temple* in Canada in which I symbolically offer flower petals, stones, prayers on paper, or whatever else I am inspired to add. I did not set out to build this unusual alter. It developed on its own and so will yours.

There are no rules.

Have fun and be free with your Sacred Space.

Be

31

Analyzing Metamorphism

Nature reveals silent transformation through isolated sanctuary within its design everywhere we observe. We can see this with the seed deep within the Earth that when ready springs forth up and out of sanctuary as a newly evolved and expanded life-form.

We can see this as a life developing in the egg that at one moment bursts forth as a new life-form. And we especially see metamorphosis through sanctuary in the example of a caterpillar turning into a butterfly. We are all familiar with this scenario but let me apply AIDS, or suffering consciousness and meditation to this example to illumine more of the love we are.

When it is time, instinct or, nature, love, life, God, the formless, etc. on some level instructs the caterpillar to create a cocoon for its evolution. And this is at a basic level is what we are doing within our sacred space. We are through stillness and observation expanding beyond

our limited thoughts and becoming a form of energetically balanced butterfly.

We are spinning a cocoon of silence to hear Love's instruction on metamorphism.

And so the caterpillar has now completed its journey and the time has come for its revolution has arrived. It could never have fathomed a life of not being a caterpillar eating leaves, crawling, and eating more leaves. Eating leaves is the life that it has known, but there is more, so much more. For deep within the caterpillar there is a connection with the infinite love that we are. This loving intelligence knows that the caterpillar will become a butterfly just at it knows at one moment we all will realize oneness. The knowing exists but not at the ego's or the caterpillar's current *level* of understanding.

This is similar to one suffering with AIDS, death, fear, or suffering consciousness. Within the intelligent consciousness of which we are integral is the knowing of who we are becoming. But at this constricted suffering *level* we are unaware of our expansion, just like the caterpillar is unaware of the clouds that it will one day soar through. So it is within our sanctuary in the stillness of the heart that we will transform into the butterfly that we always are. And this occurs through Love's grace. We only need to pause and listen. This is a love that

harmonizes all distorted consciousness, including *AIDS Consciousness*.

Realize that *things* do not grow they are eternally called home through the octaves of expanding light.

Also, please embrace the entire experience of your life, including your suffering because all is love, though much of this we do not realize.

When we suffer we need to surrender to the knowing that Love holds our most divine interest at hand. It is our limitations that have created our suffering.

When we surrender our evolving limitations and purify our consciousness we then open up to the end of our suffering.

Love

32

Meditation

Meditation is a word with so much energetic attachment to it that it is hard to hear or even type. This is analogous to stepping into a raging storm where the communication becomes strained and near impossible. As we are then yelling the simplest of instruction to another only the wind is heard, and the same is when we say the word meditation.

We instantly think of India, gurus, new agers' with robes, crystals, sandals, or who knows what else, and this then creates a division between ourselves and meditation. There are many reasons that this much energy and history is a part of the word meditation. Every person in some way has practiced a form of meditation be it in self-reflection, prayer, contemplative reading, time with nature, being lost in music, and more. The energy supply associated with meditation is incalculable and yet invaluable to discovering the truth.

When I say meditation I am speaking of observing our mind so that we realize what is going on inside of us. "What are we thinking and why? Are we more than this body? Do we really die, and then what? Where are we from? How did I develop into this person, and into the sick person that I am today? What steps have I taken that created this consciousness?" These are all valid questions that are answered through the knowing of who we are, and we find out who we are through meditation.

We know our oneness through our stopping and observing of the present.

Meditation is taking the time each day to look within into your inner-world, at who you are. Not looking at your externally formed self but the self that is without the labels of the world. You are realizing the one who exists when your physical eyes are opened or not. When we are at such a low state of energy within the world of AIDS, *AIDS Consciousness*, fear, death, or limitation consciousness we need to rapidly figure out how our energy is being spent, and meditation is a powerful way to achieve this.

I am not an expert on meditational teachings, styles, or modalities. I naturally had affinity for a few methods and it is these I will share in future writings seeing that these are my direct experience. You can go to any bookstore and find meditational paths into the heart and you will resonate and begin what you begin. All that I ask is to begin one teaching and stay with it.

As I previously stated, when I first started to meditate in 2002 it was pure chaos when I looked into my mind. I could not believe the constant flow of thoughts, beliefs, people, memories, gods, dreams, images, and just plain noise that was *on* all of the time. I could not follow one breath in and out of my body in silence, not one. So do not worry if you experience this also. Everyone will experience thoughts or inner vibratory energetic activity when they begin meditating.

And furthermore, as I attempted to observe this one breath about 20 different sounds and inner-actions occurred. I then pondered "Who am I if I am not all of these thoughts filling my head?" There was an entire world within that this *normal* consciousness was unaware of, just sort-of running chaotic in the background of my life. I remember thinking clearly, "No wonder I'm exhausted. This amount of data-flow must require an incalculable amount of energy to sustain.", and I was right.

Among my different analogous perspectives of life I have a computer-like way of looking at things as well. In that we are the human Intranet in nature's Internet. As we are born and die we are then the cosmic blood-flow of the one cosmic Love, breathing the love-breath of Love. Angels, teachers, prophets, avatars, and more are computer-like mind programs that run in creation when needed, or when they are *called*. Levels of understanding are operating systems as well as these lives that blink in and out like quick mathematical electron light-functions that are a part of larger and larger expanding operating systems, but I digress for now.

Future writings will examine in detail our consciousness and the holographic mechanisms of nature as I perceive.

Be

33

Researching to Survive

I had no idea how to meditate. I had meditated briefly in my late teens experiencing some astral colors and lucid dreams but I was young and clear. I was not so *full* of life experience or thoughts. I had not gathered up so many *things*. I had not suffered. Now I thought too much, and this thinking was doing nothing but creating new reflections in the mirror of my life to become lost in. I was clueless and flooded with too many ways on how to meditate. I did not know where, when, or how so I continued my insatiable research into life.

I had been reading books, blogs, sites, transcripts, dialogs and watching videos concerning AIDS, HIV, God, Yoga, Advaita, Vedanta, Ascended Masters, Mother Mary, Jesus, Buddhism, Zen, Christianity, Hinduism, Taoism, Indian Gurus, Pranayama, The Saints, Yoga, fasting, Sufism, nutrition, anatomy and physiology, juicing, physics, sun gazing, The Bible and other ancient and modern *spiritual* books and texts, Kundalini, the Merkaba, Pythagoras and the ancient teachers and philosophers, Platonic's, Pi, myriad energy healing systems, Shinto, Reiki, chakras, Goddess, Gaia, Tarot, crystals, ascension, enlightenment, angels, 2012, Mayans, Incans, Egyptians, Sumerians, Aztecs, Lemuria and ancient lands and cultures, channeling, Sacred Geometry, auras, you name it I was in, through, and out of it. I was seeking.

I was researching to find an understanding of myself, my disease, and to ensure my survival. I had read many *spiritual* and modern books that touched upon meditation and stillness so I did have a foundation as clouded as it was. I read books of others that I admired as *spiritual* or those we consider enlightened and knew that they meditated, prayed, or spent time with nature, and that this is a commonality amongst seekers of truth.

I also spoke in-depth with my wise and meditatively-experienced younger brother Joshua for countless hours concerning life, love, God, and meditation, and this was and *is* invaluable. But one day I realized that I was only creating more directions to wander in when what I really needed to do was just stop and sit down.

When we think there is a path then that thought "is" the path.

After a few weeks of continued research I realized I had only through my continued research added *more* to the inner-noise and this was not my goal. I was meditating and now thinking of the new facts or ideas I had just acquired on meditation and this was not helping. I was expending even more energy. My head was full, way too full. Then I somehow knew enough to stop, and so I did. I realized that all I needed to do was to be still.

Seeing that I now had *full-blown* AIDS (T-cells below 30) I had no choice but to figure out my life or lose it. I needed to heal. I had read accounts of others who had healed themselves of cancer and other diseases including AIDS, and knew that meditation was one of among many lifestyle modifications they made. I was determined. There are incredible books available on how to heal and know the body and as you deepen into yourself these may fill your shelf as they did mine.

My desire was to simplify my life and to quell the inner-noise to survive and stay sane. I stopped reading about meditation and kept sitting longer and longer in meditation and then a miracle occurred. I began to meditate.

A few months later I realized that I was meditating. I was sitting and breathing without trying to breathe or sit. I was observing. I was relaxed. I was unwound. I could breathe, and deeply without effort. I would wake up and immediately meditate as comfortably and as consistently as taking a shower, as if I had meditated my entire life. It was the most incredible and yet natural and remembered *feeling*. It was beyond a *feeling* and truly only the beginning of a journey to being awake and aware.

This concludes the introduction and beginning stages of my journey. The next chapter is a glimpse into what will be shared in future writings.

Love

34

A Visual Analogy of Awareness

Let us utilize a visual analogy to understand and *taste* awareness through meditation. In your mind's eye (or your inner vision) envision a busy street corner. This may be any corner in the world that you know, just let it contain buildings, cars, people, and nature. Now, observe a light rain beginning to fall. This is only a light drizzle of rain and let us also for this analogy realize that even though there are innumerable raindrops it is actually one rain.

As the rain continues falling observe it blanketing and washing all of the *things* in the scene. And as it continues falling the rain is washing away the colors, textures, and layers of every*thing* in the scene. The rain is like a paint-thinner revealing what is below the painted *skin* of the street-corner scene. All now in the scene appears to be of dripping wet paint.

As you continue observing you see a consistency being revealed. Under the skins and layers of the *things* in the street-corner scene is a shimmering gold. Everything is now shimmering gold. Buildings are revealed as shimmering gold. Streets and sidewalks are revealed as shimmering gold. The grass, leaves, plants and trees are also a shimmering gold. The sky and the ground are this shimmering gold. Even people are now this glorious shimmering gold.

You realize that under the layers of the reality you normally experience is this rain-revealed shimmering gold.

In this analogy the *rain* is our awareness that through meditation is expanding and revealing our oneness as an omnipresent shimmering gold.

you are that you are that you are that you are that you are that you are that you are that

There is no-thing to seek.

Thank You

Thank you so much for taking time out of your precious life to read this book. I hope that you have enjoyed this journey so far and that have made some insight into your own journey. There is much more to share.

I hope you are inspired by the sharing that we are more than the body and more than any dis-ease.

And I pray that with every breath you deepen into the joy of being aware.

We are truly free, and we realize this through gratitude and non-judgment for every experience.

Because every moment is divine no matter if we think so or not.

I wrote, edited, and self-published this book and would be humbled with any assistance in getting this book to the masses.

Love,

Richard N. Schooping

Richard
2009

Bio

Richard N. Schooping is an Inspirational Singer, Songwriter, Speaker, Artist and Author. He is also a Certified Holistic Health Consultant practicing in the Detroit, Michigan area. Richard has been married for more than thirteen years and was born and raised in Maitland, Florida, a sleepy suburb of north Orlando. Richard is now *awake.*

www.richardschooping.com

His upcoming book expounds on his suffering, his Vipassana Meditation practice, the Architecture of our Consciousness, awareness, energy, beliefs and the limitations inherent, knowing and unknowing the state of beyond, transcending fear and realizing our root-fears, the *role* of mythology and archetypes, guilt, the mechanics of prayer, *being* more than worship. It also addresses topics such as God, space, communication, imagination, knowledge, energy, sound, vibration, music, creation, evolution, gurus, dimensions, mandalas, chanting, Pi, and more.

This next book travels deep into the heart of our experience and offers insights and realizations discovered on Richard's awakening.

This book will be available 2010.

Musical CD: ***This Song We Sing*** containing 10 original songs available at www.richardschooping.com.

Richard is on Facebook.com as user "Richard Schooping"

And on Twitter.com as user "Emptyfull"

And on Linkedin.com as user Richard Schooping

Be

www.ingramcontent.com/pod-product-compliance
Lightning Source LLC
Chambersburg PA
CBHW021058090426
42738CB00006B/402

* 9 7 8 0 5 7 8 0 0 5 2 5 6 *